KU-477-427

The Whispering Island Game

based on Enid Blyton's
Five have a Mystery to Solve

Illustrated by Gary Rees

HODDER AND STOUGHTON
LONDON SYDNEY AUCKLAND TORONTO

British Library Cataloguing in Publication Data

The Whispering Island game. – (Famous Five adventure games)
   1. Games – Juvenile literature   2. Adventure and
   adventurers – Juvenile literature
   I. Series
` 793′.9   GV1203

   ISBN 0-340-36399-1

Text copyright © Stephen Thraves/ Darrell Waters Ltd 1985
Illustrations copyright © Hodder and Stoughton Ltd 1985

First published 1985
Fourth impression 1988

Published by Hodder and Stoughton Children's Books,
a division of Hodder and Stoughton Ltd,
Mill Road, Dunton Green, Sevenoaks, Kent TN13 2YJ

Photoset by Rowland Phototypesetting Ltd,
Bury St Edmunds, Suffolk

Printed in Great Britain by Hazell, Watson & Viney Ltd,
Member of BPCC plc,
Aylesbury, Bucks

You have often read about The Famous Five's adventures . . . now here's your chance to take part in one!

This time YOU are in charge. YOU have to work out the clues, read the maps, crack the codes. Whether The Five solve the mystery or not is in your hands.

You will not necessarily solve the mystery on your first attempt. It may well take several goes. Keep trying, though, and you will eventually be successful.

Even when you *have* solved the mystery, the game can still be played again. For there are many different routes to the solution – and each route involves different clues and adventures.

So the game can be played over and over. As many times as you like!

HOW TO PLAY

To solve the mystery, you have to go with The Five on an adventure through the book. You do this by starting at PARAGRAPH ONE and then following the instructions to other paragraphs.

Many of the paragraphs will ask you to work out some sort of clue. You do not have to work out every one of the clues to solve the final mystery . . . but the more you manage, the more you're likely to be successful. The less clues you crack, the less chance of completing the adventure.

To help you work out the clues, there are several pieces of equipment available – a torch, a compass, a map and a codebook. You can start with only *one* of these EQUIPMENT CARDS but you will often pick up others as the game goes along. Occasionally, however, you will be asked to give some up as well.

To hold your EQUIPMENT CARDS during the adventure, there is a RUCKSACK CARD. This will tell you exactly which EQUIPMENT CARDS you have for use at any one time (so, after they've helped in solving a particular clue, always remember to return them to your rucksack!) Any EQUIPMENT CARDS not in your rucksack **cannot be used or consulted** – and therefore should be kept out of play.

Of course, no Famous Five adventure could take place without provisions. You are therefore given three PICNIC CARDS. These are to be kept in the slit of the LUNCHBOX CARD.

Every time The Five eat or lose some of their provisions during the adventure, you must remove one of your PICNIC CARDS from the LUNCHBOX CARD. When there are no PICNIC CARDS left in your LUNCHBOX, the provisions have run out and so you cannot possibly continue with the adventure. The game is over and you will have to start again from the beginning.

READY TO START

The Famous Five are JULIAN (the biggest and eldest), DICK, GEORGE (real name Georgina, but she always wanted to be a boy), ANNE and George's dog, TIMMY.

They are spending some of their school holiday at Hill Cottage, where they are looking after a boy called Wilfrid while his grandmother visits a sick relation. The cottage is perched right on top of the cliffs and overlooks a tree-covered island a little out to sea. Wilfrid tells them that it is called Whispering Island because of the eerie noise the wind makes through the dense leaves of its trees.

They are told more about the island by Lucas, an old groundsman at the nearby golf course. He says that there was once a fine castle which contained many treasures on the island. The castle was now just a ruin, but what happened to the treasures no one ever found out. The last people to visit the island – a couple of men from a London museum – were never seen again!

Far from putting them off, it makes The Five eager to investigate the island themselves. Lucas says it would be very unwise, though, and so does Major Bullen when he comes along. He is the treasurer of the golf club and is a lot less friendly than Lucas. He tells them that the island has a bad name and they should forget all about it if they know what's good for them.

But The Five don't forget about it, immediately planning a visit to this mysterious island . . .

To join them on this visit, you will first of all need to put on your rucksack. So pick out the RUCKSACK CARD and have it near to you. You must now choose a piece of equipment to take with you. The Five each have a map, a torch, a compass and a codebook – but you can start with only *one* of these. Which do you think would be the most useful? Insert the EQUIPMENT CARD you have chosen into the slit of your RUCKSACK CARD and keep the remaining three EQUIPMENT CARDS out of play until told you can pick them up.

Now for the provisions. On returning to the cottage, Anne prepares for them a delicious picnic of sandwiches, cherry cake and ginger beer. Put the three PICNIC CARDS into the slit of your LUNCHBOX CARD. Don't forget to remove a picnic card every time The Five eat or lose some of their provisions.

Remember: When there are no PICNIC CARDS left in your LUNCHBOX, the adventure has to stop and you must start all over again.

Good Luck!

'Well, are we all ready?' asked Julian when they had checked the contents of their rucksacks. Wilfrid was much too scared of the island and so they left him to look after the cottage while they went in search of a place to hire boats. The first thing to do was to find a way down to the beach but they all had different ideas as to the best route. Even Timmy, by the sound of his noisy yap! 'I know,' said Julian when they couldn't seem to agree, 'we'll draw straws for it.' So he picked five blades of grass, hiding the ends in his fist. The one who drew the longest would be the one to choose the way!

Throw the special FAMOUS FIVE DICE to decide who it's to be – and then turn to the appropriate number. If you throw 'Mystery', you must turn to that number instead.

JULIAN thrown	go to 78
DICK thrown	go to 108
GEORGE thrown	go to 135
ANNE thrown	go to 65
TIMMY thrown	go to 121
MYSTERY thrown	go to 229

The mist finally cleared again and the island was suddenly a lot closer now. They could just hear the strange whistling sound that had given it its name. 'Ooh, isn't it eerie?' said Anne, wondering whether they should go and explore it after all. But the others said they would be perfectly safe with Timmy there. Just as he was giving her a reassuring lick, Anne spotted an old statue high up on the island's cliffs. They decided to look it up on their maps to see which part this was.

Use your MAP CARD to find out which square the statue is in – then follow the instruction. If you don't have a MAP in your RUCKSACK, you'll have to guess which instruction to follow.

If you think B4	go to 68
If you think C4	go to 186
If you think A4	go to 306

A second later, though, Timmy did an extraordinary thing. Before they had quite found their compasses, he suddenly leapt over the boat's side and into the water! 'Timmy, what are you doing?' George cried after him with alarm. 'Quick, come back to the boat – the mist will be here shortly!' But Timmy kept paddling, making for the bay. 'Oh, no, he's lost,' cried George as the mist soon enveloped both him and the boat. 'I'll never see him again!' But then they suddenly heard a series of barks and George realised what Timmy was up to. 'He's swum for shore,' she said happily, '– and now he's guiding us in by his barking. He couldn't have trusted the compass idea!' *Go to 305.*

4

Finding south-east on their compasses, they quickly measured out the 15 paces. It brought them to several small rocks embedded in the sand. 'I wonder what's special about a few rocks,' said Dick – but then George noticed that one of the rocks was a bit loose. 'This is what's so special!' she exclaimed, finding a torch underneath. 'That's what the message meant about flashing a signal,' she added, '– you could do it with this torch!' They didn't want to flash a signal just yet but they thought the torch might well come in useful as a spare and so they put it in one of their rucksacks.

If you don't already have the TORCH CARD, put it in your RUCKSACK as well. Now go to 54.

5

They had hardly decoded the first word of the message when George suddenly thought she heard someone. The others listened out as well, their hearts pounding away. 'Yes, there *is* someone!' exclaimed Julian when they heard a crackle of twigs back down the path. 'Quick, let's find somewhere to hide!' They all ran towards a clump of bushes, hurriedly crouching behind. As the noise came nearer, Julian cautiously peeped out to see who it was. 'Why, it's just a deer,' he laughed loudly, 'how stupid we all are!' The deer was surprisingly tame and so Anne fed it with some cucumber from one of her sandwiches. Now that she knew that such lovely animals lived in the forest, she was rather less scared of it!

Take one PICNIC CARD from your LUNCHBOX. Now go to 30.

They had been walking through the woods for a good hour now but the castle was still nowhere in sight. 'Let's stop for some of our picnic,' moaned George, 'I'm starving.' The others agreed, finding an old tree stump to sit on. Julian counted the stump's rings as he munched on one of his corned beef sandwiches. 'Gosh,' he said, 'this tree is more than two hundred years old!'

Take one *PICNIC CARD* from your *LUNCHBOX*. Now go to 188.

Forcing a path through the trees once more, they expected to get a glimpse of the castle at any moment now. Suddenly, though, they all froze in their tracks as they heard someone calling after them from behind. 'Don't worry,' shouted the voice, 'it's just me – Wilfrid. I decided to join your adventure after all!' They all jumped for joy as he hurried up to them, saying how lucky he was to find them in such a huge wood. Anyway, the fact was that he *had* found them and they shared some of their picnic with him to celebrate.

Take one *PICNIC CARD* from your *LUNCHBOX*. Now go to 309. (Remember: when there are no picnic cards left in your lunchbox, the game has to stop and you must start all over again.)

With the help of their compasses, they soon reached the cliff-top and they began to follow it round, looking out for the cave. 'Now don't go too near the edge, Timmy,' George warned as he bounded after the seagulls. 'We don't want you falling all the way to the bottom!' Timmy thought it was a bit unfair, though. If the seagulls could dive over the edge, then why couldn't he! *Go to 46.*

At last the cave came into view – a large black hole at the foot of the cliffs ahead. They hoped that it was the right one but then they could just make out three men standing on the narrow beach that surrounded it. As they approached, they could see that the men were piling up crates of some sort. After about half an hour of this, the men then suddenly disappeared into the cave! 'It must be the beginning of a secret tunnel,' said Julian excitedly. 'Let's try and find a way down and see where it leads!' They eventually discovered a narrow path cut into the cliff-face and they hurriedly climbed down towards the beach below. Not long after, they were approaching the eerie mouth of the cave, wondering who was to enter first . . .

Throw the FAMOUS FIVE DICE to decide.

JULIAN thrown	go to 58
DICK thrown	go to 203
GEORGE thrown	go to 87
ANNE thrown	go to 260
TIMMY thrown	go to 128
MYSTERY thrown	go to 244

Just as he was feeling for his torch, however, Julian suddenly realised that Timmy was perfectly quiet! 'It can't be rats,' he said to Anne with relief, '– if it was, Timmy would be barking his head off by now! You know how excited they make him.' Anne *did* know, remembering the fuss he made last time and so she no longer minded going without a torch. Besides, the tunnel soon came to an end at a large wooden door. They slowly turned the handle, wondering what was on the other side . . . ***Go to 245.***

On their way towards the sandy beach, Dick suddenly noticed a small book lying on the ground. Picking it up, he found that it was a secret codebook and with the name *CARLO FENZI* written on the front. 'This must belong to one of those men,' he said, '– they all looked rather foreign!' Thinking it might be useful evidence against the gang, they took it with them so they could hand it over to the police.

If you don't already have it, put the CODEBOOK CARD into your RUCKSACK. Now go to 60.

They at last reached the beach where their boat was hidden. 'We'd better hurry,' said Julian as they pushed it towards the water, 'it's beginning to get dark. It probably won't be long after nightfall that the gang's boat will come and collect the treasures!' As soon as the boat was in deep enough, they all jumped in. 'Right, who's to do the steering?' Julian asked urgently.

Throw the FAMOUS FIVE DICE to find out.

JULIAN thrown	go to 117
DICK thrown	go to 170
GEORGE thrown	go to 35
ANNE thrown	go to 62
TIMMY thrown	go to 272
MYSTERY thrown	go to 288

13

The sky seemed to be growing darker by the second and the sea had now virtually turned to black. 'Ooh, isn't it scary,' said Anne as their boat silently continued on its way, 'I don't think I've ever been on the sea at night before!' George was finding it a little scary too and she suggested switching on one of their torches to make it less spooky.

*Use your **TORCH CARD** to help light up the sea by placing exactly over the shape below – then follow the instruction. If you don't have one, go to 91 instead.*

Anne did the directing – sitting at the front with the motor-boat's pilot while the others told the sergeant in more detail what they had witnessed on their adventure. By the time they had finished, they had crossed over to the island and were now following its coastline, looking for the cave. George could just make out an old flagpost on the cliff-top and she offered to look it up on her map to find out roughly where they were.

Use your MAP CARD to find which square the flagpost is in – then follow the instruction. If you don't have one, you'll have to guess which instruction to follow.

If you think E1	go to 196
If you think D2	go to 106
If you think D1	go to 217

Having found a path down to the beach on their maps, they walked round the golf course towards it. Before they left, they made Timmy fill up his hole again and they didn't speak to him for a while to show how cross they were with him. 'Oh no, he's at it again!' cried Anne as he suddenly darted ahead and started rooting amongst the grass. It wasn't a bone he dug up this time, though, but an old book. 'Look, it seems to be some sort of codebook!' said Julian, flicking through the soiled pages, 'let's take it with us in case it might be any help.' Although they already had codebooks with them, this one looked a lot easier to use.

If you don't already have it, put the CODEBOOK CARD into your RUCKSACK. Now go to 94.

16

The mist was by now so thick, however, that both the message and their codebooks were almost impossible to read. 'I know,' said Dick, feeling through his rucksack again, 'I'll use my torch.' He had hardly switched the torch on when a large wave crashed against the boat, nearly turning it over! Fortunately, they all managed to stay in but the wave hit them with such force that Dick dropped his torch over the edge. It was now well on its way to the sea-bottom!

If you have it, remove the TORCH CARD from your RUCK-SACK. Now go to 2.

17

It was difficult to see more than a metre in front but, following their compasses, they successfully found the bay. When the water was down to only a few centimetres deep, Julian leapt out and dragged the boat well up on to the sand. 'Well, we made it!' he said as the others now jumped out of the boat as well. 'Now the adventure's *really* about to begin!' ***Go to 82.***

18

'This wood seems to grow darker at every step!' said George as she led the way. She was jolly glad that she had Timmy with her or she might well have considered turning straight round and going back to the boat! The trees all looked much the same – tall and dark – but one of them caught her notice. An arrow had been carved into the bark, pointing upwards. A little further up the trunk, there was another arrow . . . and, even higher, another! 'They must be to show that there's something up there,' she told the others excitedly. The trouble was, it was so dark above their heads that they couldn't really see properly. 'I know,' said Dick, 'let's use our torches!'

Use your torch as well by placing exactly over the shape below –
then follow the instruction. If you don't have a TORCH CARD
in your RUCKSACK, go to 220 instead.

19

'Why, it's Wilfrid!' they all exclaimed with surprise and relief as
they saw who it was. Wilfrid said that he had decided to join their
adventure after all and he had come across in another boat. 'Well,
you're very lucky to have found us in this great big wood,' said
Julian, 'but we're glad to have you with us!' Now six in their group,
they returned to the job of finding the castle. Suddenly, there was its
grey sombre shape, in a large clearing ahead! Although it was in
ruins, there was still a lot of it there – one tower almost completely
intact. They walked through an arched entrance into the inner
courtyard, wondering which part to explore first. They all had
different suggestions!

Throw the FAMOUS FIVE DICE to decide whose suggestion
they are to follow.

JULIAN thrown	go to 152
DICK thrown	go to 112
GEORGE thrown	go to 308
ANNE thrown	go to 43
TIMMY thrown	go to 259
MYSTERY thrown	go to 232

The gateway *was* shown on their maps. Unfortunately, though, they had been going the wrong way because the gateway was even further from the castle than the well had been! 'Never mind,' said Julian, having another look at his map, 'there seems to be a path here that runs directly to the castle grounds.' They hadn't been walking far along this path when they suddenly heard footsteps behind. Nervously, they turned round to see who it was. 'Wilfrid!' they all cried at once. 'What are you doing here?' Wilfrid said that he had decided to come on their adventure after all and so he had hired a boat himself to follow them. 'Well, you were jolly lucky to find us,' said Anne happily. 'You could have been searching in this wood for years!' **Go to 309.**

While she was searching for her codebook, Anne left her lunchbox on the crate. Unfortunately, her bottle of ginger beer wasn't screwed up tightly and it started to leak through the lunchbox's corners. The next time she looked, it was all over the crate! Not only was more than half her ginger beer gone, but the pencilled message had been washed out! 'I'll make sure I screw the cap on more tightly in future,' she apologised as they headed towards the cave.

Take one PICNIC CARD from your LUNCHBOX. Now go to 225.

They were just about to switch on the torch when Dick had a sudden thought. Those men might not be much further ahead and the beam of the torch could well attract their attention. He suggested they try and do without it, therefore, just feeling their way along the tunnel wall instead. 'Be careful of the floor,' Julian warned as he took the lead, 'it's very smooth and slippery.' His warning came just a fraction too late, however, because when he turned round he saw that Anne was flat on her back! Luckily, she wasn't hurt at all but she had dropped her lunchbox in the fall and her bottle of ginger beer was broken.

Take one PICNIC CARD from your LUNCHBOX. Now go to 142.

As Dick was climbing the rope, he suddenly realised where they were. 'It's the well we were at earlier!' he called back to the others. 'I can just see the winch at the top!' When he had climbed out, therefore, he decided it would be easier just to pull the others up with the handle. The only problem was Timmy – but then Julian had the brilliant idea of taking him up in his rucksack! 'Right, let's hurry back to the boat,' Dick said when they were all finally above ground again, 'we'll use Timmy to sniff out the way we came.' Just as they were about to leave the well, however, they thought they heard voices from inside. Worried that it might be the men following them, they quickly looked for their torches to shine down the hole.

Use your TORCH CARD to light up the well by placing exactly

over the shape below – then follow the instruction. If you don't have one, go to 36 instead.

24

'Do you want to swap round yet?' Dick asked Julian when he had been rowing for a good half hour and was beginning to look a bit tired. Julian said that he would continue for just a little longer. 'Well, have some of my ginger beer to refresh you,' chuckled George as she put the bottle to his mouth.

Take one PICNIC CARD from your LUNCHBOX. Now go to 13.

25

They suddenly noticed a bearded man coming towards them out of the darkness. 'What are you young children doing out so late?' he asked, introducing himself as the coastguard. Julian said that it was very important that they reached the police station and asked if he could tell them where it was. 'Well, yes, certainly,' the man replied

in surprise. 'It's about a twenty minute walk south-east from here.'
Julian thanked him, hurriedly looking for his compass.

Use your COMPASS CARD to find south-east by placing
exactly over the shape below – and with pointer touching north.
Then go to the number that appears in the window. If you don't
have one, you'll have to guess which of the numbers to go to.

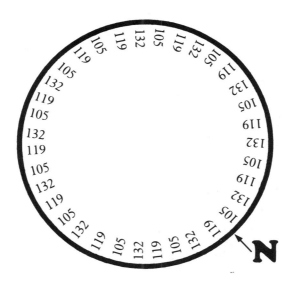

They hadn't been waiting long when they noticed several small dark
figures emerge from the cave. 'That's the gang!' George whispered
excitedly. 'We only just got here in time!' They then saw one of the
figures switch on a torch and point it out to sea, making it flash every
so often. 'It must be a signal to show their boat where to land,' said
the sergeant. Julian suddenly had an idea. By using their compasses
they could find out which direction the torch was being flashed and
that would then give them a clue as to where the boat was coming

from. So they all hurriedly started searching through their ruck-sacks.

Use your COMPASS CARD to find the direction the torch is being flashed by placing exactly over the shape below – and with pointer touching north. Then go to the number that appears in the window. If you don't have one, you'll have to guess which of the numbers to go to.

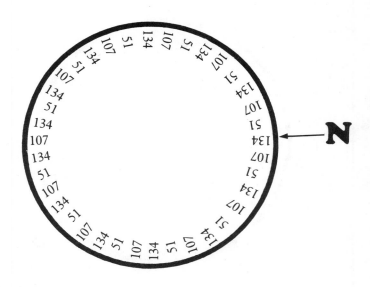

With the help of their compasses, they soon found the path Lucas had described. They were just about to start following it when Timmy sniffed out a golf-club in the long grass. 'It must belong to that man over there,' said Dick, noticing someone searching round in the distance. 'Oh, thank you,' exclaimed the man when they had taken it to him, 'I've been looking for that club everywhere.' In fact, he was so grateful that he gave them a little map of the island as a

present. 'That might come in useful on your adventures!' he said
with a wink, guessing what they were up to.

*If you don't already have it, put the MAP CARD into your
RUCKSACK. Now go to 66.*

28

'There's a bay!' Dick suddenly shouted, pointing to where the cliffs
dropped down to a small sandy part in the distance. Julian started to
row towards it but on the way George asked him to stop. 'Look at
that tree up there!' she said, pointing out a tall oak a little back from
the cliff edge. 'Someone seems to have painted a message down its
trunk!' Julian rowed a little closer so they could work out what it said
but then they realised that it was in some sort of code. 'I know,' said
Anne suddenly, just as they were starting to sigh with disappoint-
ment, 'we can use our codebooks.' So they all reached for their
rucksacks to take them out.

*Do you have a CODEBOOK in your RUCKSACK? If so, use it
to find out what the message said by decoding the instruction
below. If you don't have a CODEBOOK, go to 67 instead.*

29

Having found the boathouse on her map, George carefully put it away again so it didn't get wet. 'With the amount of spray you're making,' she said, with a poke of her tongue at Dick, 'I'd better make sure it's as far down my rucksack as possible!' Dick pretended not to hear the remark but, on the very next stroke, he hit the water with such a splash that George's face was left soaking wet. Even Timmy couldn't help a little grin! *Go to 41.*

30

They had walked quite a bit further through the wood when they spotted a small, circular wall. Coming right up to it, they saw that it was an old well. 'Perhaps this is where the people from the castle obtained their water,' suggested Julian. If it was, then it showed that the castle must be quite close now! They sat on the well's edge for a short rest but suddenly disaster struck. Anne accidentally knocked her rucksack and it fell right down the hole! They were just thinking that they would have to leave it when Dick had an idea. The well's rope was still there and so one of them could hang on to it while the others lowered him down. All they had to do now was wait for someone to volunteer!

Throw the FAMOUS FIVE DICE to decide who it's going to be.

JULIAN thrown	go to 241
DICK thrown	go to 69
GEORGE thrown	go to 83
ANNE thrown	go to 177
TIMMY thrown	go to 138
MYSTERY thrown	go to 125

31

Before they all set off, Anne asked them to wait a moment while she checked that nothing in her rucksack had been damaged. She was worried that her torch might have been broken but, when she switched it on, it worked perfectly. How lucky she was that there had been water at the bottom of that well! *Go to 291.*

32

As soon as Dick had led them to the top of the steps, they all dashed out of the castle entrance and into the wood again. They then tried to find their way to the cliffs but they were soon as lost as before. Spotting a tree with strong branches all the way up, Julian suggested that he climb to the top and see if he could glimpse the coast from up there. 'Yes, I can just see the cliff-tops!' he shouted down to the others through the leaves. So they would know which direction to go, he took the compass from his pocket. It was a good job Anne had reminded him to take it with him!

Use your COMPASS CARD to check the cliffs' direction by placing exactly over the shape below – and with pointer touching north. Then go to the number that appears in the window. If you don't have one, you'll have to guess which of the numbers to go to.

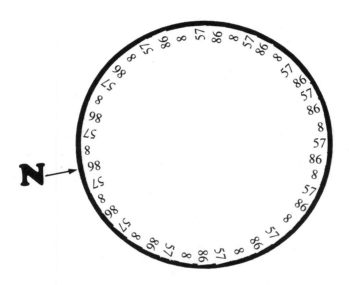

33

While looking for his compass, Dick had taken the map from his rucksack and momentarily put it on the ground. Suddenly, though, there was a large gust of wind across the castle ruins and it whisked the map up into the air. They all rushed after it across the courtyard, worried that it might be carried up on to a high ledge and become impossible to reach. Instead, however, it suddenly dropped through a hole in the ground! 'Look, it's a downward stairway,' exclaimed George when they had come up to the hole and saw some dark steps inside. 'It looks like we've found the entrance to the dungeons without our compasses!' As for poor old Dick's map, though, that was ruined. It had fallen into a deep puddle of water on the fifth step down and was now a soggy mess!

If you have one, take the MAP CARD from your RUCKSACK. Now go to 201.

34

They now started to enter the cave. 'Gosh, it's vast!' exclaimed Dick, staring up at the high, dark roof. The others told him to keep his voice down, however. It was making such a loud echo that it might be heard by the men! ***Go to 313.***

35

George said that *she* would do the steering so the boys could share the rowing. Normally she would insist on rowing herself – to try and prove that she was just as fast as the boys – but since this was so urgent, it seemed no time for showing off. *Secretly*, she knew that she was a good bit slower than them! They had rowed quite a distance from the beach when they spotted a statue on the cliff-top. Anne suggested they look it up on their maps to find out how much further they had to go.

Use your MAP CARD to find which square the statue is in – then follow the instruction. If you don't have one, you'll have to guess which instruction to follow.

If you think A3	go to 246
If you think A4	go to 13
If you think B4	go to 181

36
While they were still looking for their torches, however, they suddenly heard a loud woof from down the well. And it came just after Timmy had given a woof himself! 'Oh, how silly we all are!' George exclaimed. 'Those voices were obviously just an echo of ourselves!' They were in such a hurry to get moving again after this delay that Julian forgot to repack his map. It was only when it was far too far to go back for it that he realised!

If you have it, remove the MAP CARD from your RUCKSACK. Now go to 60.

37
The coded message did indeed have something to do with the island! It said that the treasures were still on the island but some evil guards patrolled it to keep snoopers away. 'I wouldn't mind betting it was written by one of those men from the museum who went missing,' said Anne excitedly as they read the message again. Perhaps it was their last act before the guards caught them and silenced them forever! Both excited and a little scared, they all felt that they were at the beginning of a *real* adventure now! *Go to 2.*

Dick volunteered to direct the way, since he thought he could remember it best. The pilot went at top speed and it wasn't long before they had reached the island, following its coastline. 'We're getting very near now,' said Dick and the sergeant ordered the pilot to go much slower so they didn't miss it. Suddenly, however, everything went into darkness! 'Oh no,' exclaimed the sergeant, 'our spotlight's bulb has gone! It will waste too much time to fit a spare.' Julian then had an idea. They could simply shine one of their torches instead!

*Use your **TORCH CARD** to light up the rest of the way by placing exactly over the shape below – then follow the instruction. If you don't have one, go to 162 instead.*

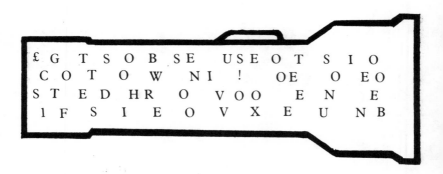

£ G   T   S   O   B   SE   USE   O   T   S   I   O
  C   O   T   O   W   NI   !   OE   O   E O
S   T   E   D   H R   O   V O O   E   N   E
 1 F   S   I   E   O   V   X   E   U   N   B

'Yes, there it is!' exclaimed George, pointing to a little symbol on her map with the words *INTREPID'S ANCHOR* written underneath. '*Intrepid* must have been the name of the ship that the anchor came from,' said Julian. But the others were more interested in seeing whether the anchor was on the way to the beach or not. 'Yes, all we have to do is follow the path for about another half mile,' said Dick, running his finger along a thin yellow line. As they were putting their maps away again, Anne noticed something gleaming in the short grass. 'Look, someone has dropped their compass!' she said, picking it up. Although they already had compasses with them, they decided to take this one as well in case they needed a spare. Besides, there was no point in just letting it go rusty!

If you don't already have it, put the COMPASS CARD into your RUCKSACK. Now go to 66.

40

Just as they were about to take their torches out, however, they heard a loud crash from inside the grotto. It sounded as if some of the roof was caving in! 'We had better leave it,' said Julian disappointedly. 'If one of those rocks hits our boat, we'll be sunk.' So he backed the boat out into the sea again, continuing towards the small bay further up. *Go to 176.*

41

The island was coming a lot closer now and they all gave a little shiver as they heard the weird whistling sound that gave it its name. 'No wonder everyone stays well clear of it!' said Julian as he looked up at the spooky trees just back from its steep cliffs. On the very next dip into the water, his oar suddenly hit something floating by. At first it looked just like an ordinary piece of wood but then Anne noticed that there was some writing on it. They fished it out to have a better look but, unfortunately, the writing was in some sort of code. 'Perhaps our codebooks will be able to help,' said George, suddenly remembering that Wilfrid had lent them one each.

*Use your **CODEBOOK CARD** to find out what the writing on the wood said by decoding the instruction below. If you don't have one in your **RUCKSACK**, go to 96 instead.*

42

The message said that they were to beware of the trap 50 metres further along the path. So they walked very cautiously for the next few minutes, studying the ground in front. Timmy suddenly made them stop, sniffing at some fallen branches. 'It looks as if this is it,' said Julian, lifting one of the branches up with his foot. He was right! Underneath there was a deep pit. 'Whoever else is on this island obviously doesn't like strangers!' Dick remarked as they all stepped carefully round it. ***Go to 30.***

They all followed Anne to a little stone tower, shaped a bit like a pottery kiln. Inside, they noticed that there were lots of holes in the roof. 'This was probably for keeping doves or pigeons,' commented Julian '– so the people in the castle would have some fresh meat.' George then pointed out that the holes would be an excellent place for hiding the treasure. The trouble was that they were so high up and it was so dark that it was difficult to see into them. It looked like a job for their torches!

Use your TORCH CARD to light up the holes by placing exactly over the shape below – then follow the instruction. If you don't have one, go to 311 instead.

They had only been following their compasses for a few minutes or so when they heard a loud cry behind. Rather cautious, they went back to investigate. Who could it possibly be? 'Wilfrid!' they all exclaimed at once on seeing him sprawled across the ground. Wilfrid said that he had decided to join their adventure after all but had tripped on a creeper across the path. Fortunately, he hadn't broken any bones and they soon helped him to his feet. 'It was probably a good job you did trip and cry out,' chuckled Dick, 'or we might never have found each other!' *Go to 309.*

Quickly following Anne to the top of the steps, they then dashed across the castle courtyard and back into the wood. They eventually spotted an old lighthouse through the trees and they hurried towards it, realising they had found the cliff-tops again. They were just about to start following the cliffs round to look out for the cave below, when George noticed a painted message at the base of the lighthouse. They went to see what it said. 'Oh, what a nuisance,' said Dick, 'it seems to be in some sort of code! Let's hope our codebooks can help.' So they quickly started to search for them in their rucksacks.

Use your CODEBOOK CARD to find out what the message said by decoding the instruction below. If you don't have one, go to 140 instead.

They finally spotted the cave – a large black hole at the foot of the cliffs below. There was a small beach around the cave and they could just make out three men there. They seemed to be piling up crates at the cave's entrance. When the work was at last finished, the men suddenly disappeared! 'The cave must be a secret tunnel to somewhere,' said Dick with excitement in his eyes. 'Let's try and find a way down and see where it goes!' They looked along the cliff edge for some sort of path, finally discovering a series of steps cut into the rock! 'This is obviously an alternative approach to the cave,' said Julian as they prepared to climb down, '– probably made by the same people who dug out the passage!'

Throw the FAMOUS FIVE DICE to decide who is to go first down the steps.

JULIAN thrown	go to 223
DICK thrown	go to 156
GEORGE thrown	go to 72
ANNE thrown	go to 212
TIMMY thrown	go to 141
MYSTERY thrown	go to 269

47

They followed their compasses to the very back of the cave. 'I can't see any tunnel,' said Wilfrid as they stared at the seemingly solid wall of rock in front of them. Suddenly, though, the hair on Timmy's back started rippling and they realised that there was a draught of air from somewhere! On examining the rock closer this time, they found a narrow gap in it – just big enough for someone to squeeze through. 'This is it,' exclaimed Julian as he led the way, 'this is the tunnel!' *Go to 262.*

Anxious to get out of the tunnel as quickly as possible, Anne offered to go first! 'Guess where we are?' she called back excitedly when she had reached the top. 'It's the well where we were before!' Next Dick went up the rope, then Wilfrid, then George. Last went Julian – carrying Timmy in his rucksack! 'Right, let's hurry back to our boat,' he said as soon as he had clambered over the little circular wall. The others wondered which direction to go but Julian reminded them that they had landed on the west side of the island. So all they had to do was follow west on their compasses!

Use your COMPASS CARD to find where west is by placing exactly over the shape below – and with pointer touching north. Then go to the number that appears in the window. If you don't have one, you'll have to guess which of the numbers to go to.

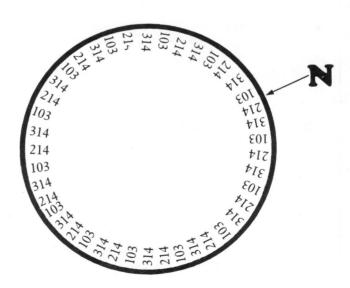

It was so windy at the top of the cliffs, however, that it was difficult to keep their maps still. 'It's probably getting too dark to read them anyway!' said George, finally giving up with hers. The others gave up with theirs too and they all had some of Julian's sandwiches while they considered what to do next.

Take one PICNIC CARD from your LUNCHBOX. Now go to 25.

Finding south on the compass, the girls told Dick which way to steer. 'A little bit to the left,' said George. 'Now a little bit to the right,' said Anne. The boat was finally pointing the right direction and they told him just to keep the rudder steady from then on. They had all been in such a hurry to row out the boat that it was only now they noticed Timmy. He seemed to be carrying a small book in his mouth. 'Look,' exclaimed Wilfrid, taking it from him, 'it's someone's codebook. He must have picked it up on the beach!'

If you don't already have it, put the CODEBOOK CARD into your RUCKSACK. Now go to 13.

The gang's motor-boat soon became visible, charging through the waves. They all watched breathlessly as it suddenly reduced its speed and headed towards the cave. 'We'll wait until it's fully stopped,' the sergeant whispered, '– then we'll make our move!' A few seconds later, they saw the boat's anchor being dropped and the men on the shore starting to carry the crates towards it. 'Right – *now!*' the sergeant shouted and his pilot suddenly switched on the engine, steering right at the gang's boat to cut it off. Realising that he was probably the gang's leader, The Five all stared into the boat's cabin to see who was at the wheel.

Use your CODEBOOK CARD to find out who it was by decoding the answer below. If you don't have one, go to 147 instead.

When they had decoded the writing on the signpost, they found that it did indeed point the way down to the beach. *BEACH – 2 MILES*, the decoded letters said. 'I wonder why the signposts haven't been replaced with new ones?' Dick asked on the way. Julian said that they were probably kept for historical interest. 'Anyway, I think it makes it a lot more exciting when they're in code,' he added. The others all agreed! *Go to 94.*

Just as they were about to take their torches out, however, Julian suddenly thought of something . . . which made it not such a good idea after all! If someone on the mainland *did* signal back, and the person on the island saw that one *as well as the light from The Five*, then they might become suspicious. So he suggested it would be wiser to put their torches back again. The less suspicion they aroused on this adventure, the better! ***Go to 41.***

Next, they walked to the far end of the beach, where they had noticed a small cave. 'Perhaps that will be a good place to hide our boat,' said Julian as he led the way. Peering through the entrance, though, he found that it was very deep and dark. 'We'll have to use our torches,' he told the others. 'I can barely see a thing!'

Use your TORCH as well by placing exactly over the shape below – then follow the instruction. If you don't have a TORCH CARD in your RUCKSACK, go to 110 instead.

```
Y G   S N   O   E @ N P G   V   T   E   N   O
  Q   T   O   H Z   £ R   N     E   D E     Q P F
C   P F   J T W     I D V   E     O   U R @
  S     T   P   H  I   R  X   E     Z   E C
```

Having spotted the graveyard on their maps, they started to study some of the stones to see how old they were. 'Look at this one,' called George, pointing to a cross marked *SIR ROLAND MANDER-VILLE*, 'it's dated 1693.' Dick found one even older, dated 1658. 'And they're all Mandervilles,' noticed Julian, '– they must have been the family who owned the castle.' Finding the ancient graveyard a little eerie, they soon continued on their way. ***Go to 188.***

56

It wasn't long before they spotted a large structure through the trees ahead and they hurried towards it, thinking it was the castle. But as it became clearer, they realised it wasn't the castle at all but a huge gateway. 'It certainly looks as old as the castle,' remarked Julian, examining the crumbling stones. 'Perhaps it was the entrance to a park just outside the castle,' he added, '– where they exercised their horses, for instance.' He then thought there was a chance of it being shown on their maps and so they all started looking through their rucksacks for them.

*Use your **MAP CARD** to find which square the old stone gateway is in – then follow the instruction. If you don't have one, you'll have to guess which instruction to follow.*

If you think B3	go to 7
If you think B1	go to 99
If you think B2	go to 20

57

When Julian had joined the others at the bottom again, however, he couldn't remember what the reading on his compass was! They decided it would waste too much time for him to climb all the way to the top again and so they would just have to guess the direction. Fortunately, they made a good guess because they soon came out at the cliff-top. They started to follow it round, looking out for the cave. On the way, Anne opened her lunchbox to check how many sandwiches she had left. But before she could close it again, a cheeky gull swooped down and pinched some of her cake.

Take one PICNIC CARD from your LUNCHBOX. Now go to 46.

58

It became darker and darker as Julian led them into the heart of the cave. Soon there was only a thin stream of light filtering through the hole. There was just enough of it, however, to show up a collection of pebbles lying around the cave's rocky floor. To begin with, they didn't really pay them much attention but then Anne realised that they were arranged to form strange letters and symbols. 'It looks like a coded message,' said Dick excitedly, beginning to look for his codebook, 'and I wouldn't mind betting it says where to find the start of the tunnel!'

*Use your **CODEBOOK CARD** to find out what the message said by decoding the instruction below. If you don't have one, go to 178 instead.*

CJZV

59

When they had found the cliff steps on their maps, they marked the area with a large cross. 'Now if we need to tell the police about those steps,' said Julian as he put his map away again, 'we'll know exactly where to direct them!' They were just about to start moving again when Wilfrid noticed a small book being blown from ledge to ledge above them. It slowly came down to within reach of Dick's hand. 'Why, it's a codebook!' he exclaimed, making a grab for it. 'It must have been dropped by one of those men.' They decided to take it with them so the owner wouldn't be able to find it again!

If you don't already have it, put the CODEBOOK CARD into your RUCKSACK. Now go to 270.

60

They at last reached the beach where their boat was hidden, quickly pushing it into the water. 'We'd better hurry,' said Julian, as he took the oars, 'it's beginning to get dark. It probably won't be long after nightfall that the gang will come in their boat and collect the treasures!' He rowed as hard as he could and then when he was tired Dick took over. 'Not much further now,' said George as the twinkling lights from the mainland came closer and closer. They could finally hear the scrape of the shore on the boat's bottom and they all dragged it high up on to the sand. 'We'll return it to the boat-keeper tomorrow,' Julian said. 'We must hurry along to the police station first!' But how did they find the police station? They all had different ideas.

Throw the FAMOUS FIVE DICE to decide whose idea they should follow.

JULIAN thrown	go to 264
DICK thrown	go to 227
GEORGE thrown	go to 247
ANNE thrown	go to 144
TIMMY thrown	go to 194
MYSTERY thrown	go to 215

Dick's rucksack was packed right at the bottom of the boat, however, and it took him quite a while to pull his codebook out. By the time he had returned to the others, the message had gone! 'A large wave just came in,' George explained to him, 'and washed it away!' There wasn't time to be disappointed about it, though, and they all hurried back to the boat. It was only when they had rowed well out to sea that Anne realised she had left her lunchbox behind on the beach!

Take one PICNIC CARD from your LUNCHBOX. Now go to 76.

62

Anne said that she would do the steering so the others could all take it in turns to do the rowing. She knew there wasn't much point in doing the rowing herself because she would be far too slow. The sky seemed to be growing darker by the second and it was becoming more and more difficult to see. 'We'd better switch on one of our torches,' said Julian, 'in case there are any dangerous rocks about.'

Use your TORCH CARD to help light up the sea by placing exactly over the shape below – then follow the instruction. If you don't have one, go to 206 instead.

```
  G   S   K   O   M   S  £X      E L      T    O    S     O
 T   N     £T C T   H    W B O   E N          S  E
 Q    A  F     O N    E U E Q R     E    N  S
   F I      C E    S   N D   I   V   A       H E    X B
```

Dick was right! The coded message *did* tell the gang's boat where to land, saying that it should go round to the cave on the other side of the island. 'I imagine the message will be set alight about half an hour or so before the boat is expected,' said Julian. 'Let's hope that's not too soon or we won't be able to reach the police in time!' ***Go to 13.***

George's map showed that the graveyard was only two bends before the cave and so they should be reaching it at any moment now. 'There it is!' shouted Dick excitedly as he spotted its dark, sinister mouth only a little way ahead. The pilot dimmed the boat's lights and switched off its engine as they all waited for something to happen. 'Let's just hope it hasn't happened already!' remarked the sergeant tensely. ***Go to 26.***

Since Anne picked the longest blade of grass, they all agreed on her idea – to head for an old signpost in the distance. 'One arm will probably point the way down to the beach,' she said as they set off towards it. When they reached the signpost, however, they noticed that the writing didn't make sense. 'How odd!' exclaimed Julian, 'it seems to be in some sort of code.' Then Anne remembered Wilfrid saying that a lot of the older signposts in this area were in code. It dated back to the days when smugglers used these cliffs and they didn't want the authorities to find their way around. The Five now realised why Wilfrid had lent them all codebooks and hurriedly searched for them in their rucksacks!

Do you have a CODEBOOK in your RUCKSACK? If so, use it to find out what the signpost said by decoding the instruction below. (Remember to put the CARD back in your RUCKSACK afterwards.) If you don't have a CODEBOOK CARD, go to 79 instead.

66

When they finally reached the beach, they immediately started looking for the boathouse. Timmy wanted them to stop to buy some ice-cream but George told him there wasn't time. 'Anyway, you would only get it all over your nose!' she added with a laugh. Dick suddenly spotted some oars resting against a hut in the distance and they hurried towards it. 'We would like to hire a boat for the whole day,' they all said excitedly to the owner. When he had paid him the money, Julian pushed the boat slightly out to sea before jumping in with the others.

Throw the FAMOUS FIVE DICE to decide who is to sit at the back and do the steering.

JULIAN thrown	go to 266
DICK thrown	go to 230
GEORGE thrown	go to 164
ANNE thrown	go to 198
TIMMY thrown	go to 122
MYSTERY thrown	go to 149

67

Just as they were opening their codebooks, however, there was a loud thud at the bottom of the boat. They had hit a rock! Fortunately, the boat wasn't damaged but it caused such a jolt that Anne let go of her rucksack. Julian was just able to catch hold of one of the straps in time before it fell into the water but he couldn't stop her compass falling out. Anne sadly watched it sink into the blackness below. Julian decided they had better forget about trying to decode the message on the tree in case they hit anything else!

If you have it, remove the COMPASS CARD from your RUCKSACK. Now go to 176.

68

Their maps showed that the statue was on the south of the island. 'Now, let's look to see if there's anywhere suitable to land nearby,' said Julian, running his finger along the coastline on the map. 'Yes, here's a likely place,' he remarked, noticing an area of beach just round the next bend. So they started to row in that direction, the beach's gold-coloured sand soon coming into sight. *Go to 82.*

Since it was Dick's idea, he thought *he* had better volunteer! He made a large knot at the end of the rope for somewhere to rest his feet and then the others carefully lowered him down. It soon became so dark inside the well, however, that he couldn't see anything. 'You had better pull me back,' he shouted up the hole, 'this is going to need a torch!' While she helped Julian and Anne turn the winch, George told Timmy to fetch a torch from one of their rucksacks. He immediately obeyed, running over to where the rucksacks rested against a tree.

Use your TORCH CARD to help Dick see by placing exactly over the shape below – then follow the instruction. If you don't have one in your RUCKSACK, go to 98 instead.

```
S G   NT  O   HR   G J E   T    T   TSN O
K V   T   HL   MR   W £ O   N K         E E
  S  M I      EV   ESE ( ) X L J   E !  T  N
&  V  F   I     O ? N    U    E :       £ V|K R E
```

At that very moment, though, the hook suddenly stopped swinging as if it had caught something. They quickly pulled the rope up, eager to see if it was the rucksack. 'It's just like fishing!' Dick remarked excitedly as there was only a little bit more to come. Finally, the hook appeared and on the end was – yes – Anne's rucksack! The excitement had been so much that they all had a quick gulp of ginger beer for their dry throats before leaving.

Take one PICNIC CARD from your LUNCHBOX. Now go to 113.

'Ooh, let's go,' said Anne, as their feet made a horrible echoing sound, 'I don't like it!' Just as the others were deciding the same, George noticed some large boxes in the corner. 'I've found the treasures!' she cried, discovering hundreds of gold plates and other precious items inside. The others hardly had time to look themselves when they heard two men's voices coming down the steps. 'Quick, behind one of the boxes!' Julian ordered as the voices grew nearer. *Go to 155.*

George carefully made her way down the steps, the others right behind. They kept as near to the cliff-face as possible so they weren't blown over by the strong wind. 'Make sure you keep an eye on Timmy,' George called back over her shoulder, '– he's a lot lighter than any of us!' She had only gone a few steps further when her hand felt some writing carved into the rock. When they tried to work out what it said, however, they realised that it was in some sort of code. They would have to take out their codebooks!

Use your CODEBOOK CARD to find out what the message said by decoding the instruction below. If you don't have one, go to 234 instead.

73

Dick was right – the coded message *did* tell them where to find the start of the tunnel! They were told to walk to the far end of the cave and then feel for a small draught of air. 'Look, here it is!' cried Dick suddenly. 'It's coming from a narrow gap in the rock!' Squeezing through the gap, they found themselves at the beginning of a long, narrow passage. 'I hope this is the right one and that message wasn't put there to deceive people,' said Julian. He suddenly had the horrible thought that the tunnel might not have an end, just twisting further and further into the cliffs. But then Timmy sniffed out a map on the ground – obviously dropped by one of the men – and so they knew this was the route they had taken after all!

If you don't already have it, put the MAP CARD into your RUCKSACK. Now go to 262.

74

When they had found the south side of the cavern with their compasses, they waited for the voices to move away and then started to examine the rock. 'Hey, come over here,' Dick suddenly whispered to the others, 'this part isn't real rock at all but just cardboard made to look like rock.' They managed to prise some of the cardboard away, discovering that it was glued to the back of a door! It even had a hole for a key. Luckily, though, the door hadn't been locked on this occasion and they slowly pushed it open, wondering where they would come out . . . *Go to 245.*

75

'There's no need to use your compasses,' the fisherman told them just as they were opening them up. 'Since you're in such a hurry, I'll take you to the place myself.' Running as fast as he was able, he led them along the beach a little and then pointed out some narrow wooden steps climbing all the way up the cliff. To show their gratitude, George gave him a large piece of her cake before he left them. 'Thank you very much,' he said, 'and be careful how you go. Those steps can be very slippery.'

Take one PICNIC CARD from your LUNCHBOX. Now go to 145.

They could at last see the lights of the mainland ahead and they knew there wasn't much further to go now. Julian decided to have one last energetic burst at the oars! Not long after, they were dragging the boat up on to the beach and making their way towards the cliff-top. They then asked Wilfrid if he knew where the police station was. 'I think it's somewhere near the pay-telescope,' he replied and so they all quickly searched for their maps to find out how to get there.

Use your MAP CARD to find which square the telescope is in – then follow the instruction. If you don't have one, you'll have to guess which instruction to follow.

If you think E4	go to 119
If you think E2	go to 161
If you think E3	go to 195

Guided by The Five's compasses, the boat was soon approaching the cave. They only went a little nearer before the sergeant ordered the boat to be stopped and its lights to be dimmed. 'We'll wait here where we can't be seen,' he said as they all stared across the water at the cave's dark, sinister entrance. It surely wouldn't be long now before something started to happen! *Go to 93.*

Julian was left with the longest blade of grass himself and so it was *his* choice they all agreed on – taking a small path along the cliff-top. 'Now not too near the edge!' George warned Timmy as he bounded excitedly along in the sunshine. They had been following the path for quite a time now but it still hadn't dropped down to the beach. Julian was beginning to worry that it didn't go that way after all and so he decided to look out for something to check on the map. 'How about that large anchor over there,' suggested Dick, pointing ahead, 'it appears to be some sort of monument.' They all searched for their maps in their rucksacks, hoping that the monument was important enough to be shown.

Do you have a MAP in your RUCKSACK? If so, use it to find out which square the anchor-monument is in – then follow the instruction. (Remember to put the CARD back in your RUCK-SACK afterwards.) If you don't have a MAP CARD, you'll have to guess which instruction to follow.

If you think D4	go to 39
If you think E2	go to 238
If you think E3	go to 66

Just as they were about to decode the writing on the signpost, however, it suddenly began to rain. 'We had better leave it,' said Julian, 'or our codebooks are going to be ruined. And we might well need them for later on.' So, putting up their anorak hoods, they decided they would just have to find their way down to the beach by pot luck. After they had been walking for about a quarter of an hour, the rain suddenly stopped again and so they decided to have a little of their picnic to celebrate.

Take one PICNIC CARD from your LUNCHBOX. Now go to 94.

'I wonder how much further it is?' asked Dick when they had been rowing for what must have been a good half hour now. Just as he was speaking, he noticed a strange glow coming from his rucksack. They had all wedged the rucksacks into the far end of the boat so they wouldn't fall out and Dick's was at the top. Anne carefully slid towards it and looked inside. 'Oh no!' she cried. 'You've left your torch on, Dick, and the batteries look as if they won't last much longer.' She was right. A second or two later and the torch gave one last flicker and went out!

If you have it, remove the TORCH CARD from your RUCK-SACK. Now go to 41.

The message said that only rowing-boats should try and land on the island because anything deeper would be cut to pieces by the sharp rocks just below the surface. It seemed a very useful warning but Anne wondered why the person responsible hadn't written it in plain English so that everyone could understand it. 'He probably didn't *want* everyone to understand it!' Dick realised with sudden horror. 'Just his friends – who I dare say would use the same code. As for everybody else, he was probably quite happy for them to be wrecked so that he could keep his island private!' *Go to 176.*

After hiding the boat behind some bushes just back from the beach, they prepared to start the exploration of the island. In front of them they could see nothing but wood – dark and menacing – but Julian was sure there must be the remains of the castle somewhere. 'Look, there's a little path over there!' said Anne, pointing to a rough track that forced its way through the trees. 'Perhaps that will lead somewhere?' They went up to where the path started, pausing for a moment to decide who should go first.

To find out, throw the FAMOUS FIVE DICE, then turn to the appropriate number.

JULIAN thrown	go to 151
DICK thrown	go to 97
GEORGE thrown	go to 18
ANNE thrown	go to 240
TIMMY thrown	go to 166
MYSTERY thrown	go to 251

83

Keen to prove that she was the bravest of The Five – except perhaps for Timmy – it was George who volunteered. Julian wasn't sure that he should let her but then he thought it would be better for a lighter person to go down. That way, it would make turning the well's handle a lot easier for the others. George eventually found the rucksack but on the way up again she suddenly shouted to the others to stop turning. She had noticed a coded message inscribed into one of the damp bricks. Memorising it, she then called to the others to have one of their codebooks ready so that she could work out the message as soon as she returned to the top.

Use your CODEBOOK CARD to work out what the message

said by decoding the instruction below. *If you don't have one, go to 252 instead.*

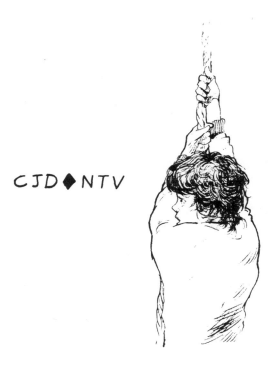

C J D ◆ N T V

84

The message said that the well was also an escape route! The others wondered what this meant, thinking it didn't make any sense. 'Escape route to where?' asked Julian, scratching his head. They couldn't spend all day puzzling about it, though, and so they started on their way again. ***Go to 113.***

85

They were just opening their codebooks when Timmy started to become rather anxious, tugging at George's sleeve. To begin with, they wondered what was wrong with him but then they realised – there were voices coming down the steps! Anne spotted some large crates in the corner and they hurried over to them to hide. Just before crouching down, Dick saw that the crates were packed with gleaming gold plates and goblets. 'Gosh, it's the treasures,' he exclaimed, 'we've found them!' Before anyone else could comment on them, though, two mean-looking men appeared . . . *Go to 155.*

86

They were so tired by the time they came out at the cliffs that they agreed to stop for a quick rest. 'Oh, isn't it nice to see the sun again!' Anne exclaimed as they lay in the short grass a safe distance from the edge. After having a little of their picnic, they started up again, deciding to follow the cliffs round until they spotted the cave.

Take one PICNIC CARD from your LUNCHBOX. Now go to 46.

87

'Make sure you all stay right behind me!' George said nervously as she led them into the heart of the cave. She kept putting her hand behind to feel Timmy's head. She had only gone a few cautious steps further when she heard a piece of paper crackle under her feet. She held it up to the thin beam of light that filtered into the cave, noticing there was a message on it. *FOR SECRET TUNNEL*, it read, *WALK SOUTH-EAST FROM DARK POOL*. They looked around them for a while, suddenly spotting a deep well of water in the cave floor. 'It must be that!' exclaimed Dick, beginning to look for his compass.

Use your COMPASS CARD to find south-east from the pool by

placing exactly over the shape below – and with pointer touching north. Then go to the number that appears in the window. If you don't have one, you'll have to guess which of the numbers to go to.

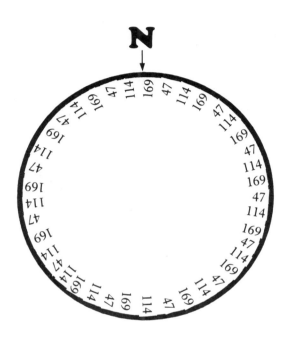

'If Wilfrid's cottage is *here*,' said Julian, pointing to where they had found it on their maps, 'then the cave must be about *here*.' His finger now pointed to a little dent shown in the island. The others all agreed that that was roughly where the cave must be, then put their maps away again. After another five or six minutes of sitting on the sand, they realised they couldn't put it off any longer. It was about time they started exploring the cave! ***Go to 225.***

Putting their maps away once more, they gingerly started to explore the cave. It made a horrible echoing noise whenever anyone spoke. Wilfrid could feel a draught of air right at the back and he went over to it, discovering a large hole in the rock. 'Look, it's the tunnel,' he called to the others, 'this is where it starts!' Walking in single file, they carefully followed the tunnel through the cliffs. It seemed to lead on and on but it finally came to an end at a large wooden door. They slowly turned the handle, wondering where they would come out . . . *Go to 245.*

Reaching the top of the shaft, Julian suddenly realised what it was. It was the well where they had stopped before! As soon as he had climbed out, he started to wind the rope, pulling the others up one by one. Timmy was the most trouble because he could only hang on by his teeth but, with George giving him a hand, he finally made it to the top. 'Now let's hurry back to our boat,' said Julian. 'We'll use Timmy to pick up our scent from before.' Timmy hadn't led them far through the wood when he sniffed out a diary on the ground. Opening it up, they saw that there was a coded message inside and so they hurriedly looked for their codebooks.

Use your CODEBOOK CARD to find out what the message said by decoding the instruction below. If you don't have one, go to 204 instead.

But Dick was worried that the gang's boat might be nearby and they would be seen if they used a torch. 'So we'd better try and do without one,' he told the girls. They didn't mind too much now, anyway, because they could at last see the lights of the mainland ahead. It wasn't long after that they were dragging the boat up on to the shore and then hurriedly following Wilfrid's directions to the police station. Julian threw out some of his sandwiches for the birds on the way to make his lunchbox easier to carry.

Take one PICNIC CARD from your LUNCHBOX. Now go to 119. (Remember: when there are no picnic cards left in your lunchbox, the game is over and you must start again.)

Just at that moment, though, the moon came out from behind a cloud and they didn't need their torches to read the signpost after all. One arm directed to the church . . . another to the path they had just used . . . and the third *to the police station!* 'It must be that building over there!' cried George pointing to where a tiny blue light was shining in the distance. As they hurried towards the police station, Julian threw out some of his sandwiches for the gulls to make his lunchbox lighter.

Take one PICNIC CARD from your LUNCHBOX. Now go to 119. (Remember: when there are no picnic cards left in your lunchbox, the game is over and you must start again.)

They suddenly saw three or four small dark figures emerge from the cave. 'That's them,' George whispered with excitement, 'they're the members of the gang!' Knowing that their boat would be coming any minute to collect them, the sergeant quickly worked out his plan. When the boat arrived, they would suddenly start up their own engine again and head for the cave themselves. To make sure the gang didn't spot them too early, however, they would have to keep their lights off and so he asked the children if they could lend the pilot a torch to help him see the controls.

Use your TORCH CARD to assist the pilot by placing exactly over the shape below. If you don't have one, go to 120 instead.

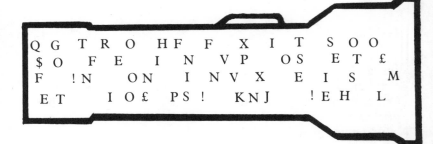

```
Q G  T R O   HF  F   X   I T    S  O O
$ O   F E    I   N   V P    O S   E T  £
F   ! N   O N   I N V X    E   I   S      M
E T     I O £  P S !    K N J     ! E H    L
```

When they at last reached the beach, they looked all round for the boathouse. 'There it is!' exclaimed Dick, pointing to a painted wooden hut a little further along. 'We would like to hire a boat for the whole day,' they said to the man in charge, and they were soon excitedly rowing out to sea. First Julian had a go at the oars, then Dick, then George, then Julian again. They were drawing right up to the island now but this part was all steep cliff and it was impossible to land. 'We'll have to look for a bay somewhere,' said Julian. 'I'll keep following the coast until one of us spots one.'

Throw the FAMOUS FIVE DICE to decide who it's to be.

JULIAN thrown	go to 185
DICK thrown	go to 28
GEORGE thrown	go to 219
ANNE thrown	go to 239
TIMMY thrown	go to 197
MYSTERY thrown	go to 297

95

'I must say, rowing's a lot harder than being towed!' remarked Dick as they followed their compasses' direction. On the other hand, though, there were certain advantages in a rowing-boat. For one, there was less chance of being heard when they landed. If there *was* something unpleasant on the island like everyone seemed to think, the quieter they were, the better! ***Go to 41.***

96

The piece of wood was so soft and rotten, however, that before they could take their codebooks out it had crumbled in their hands! 'What a shame!' said Julian. 'It might have been something important.' They soon returned their interest to the island, though, and how they were going to land. To begin with, it looked as if it was impossible – there being nothing but steep cliffs – but then Timmy spotted a small, sandy beach just before the next bend. 'Well done, Timmy!' cried the others. 'For that, you can have a nice piece of cherry cake.'

Take one PICNIC CARD from your LUNCHBOX. Now go to 82.

97

The whistling of the trees grew louder and louder as Dick led them further and further in. 'Ooh, isn't it horrible!' exclaimed Anne. 'It sounds like lots of people chattering to each other.' But Julian said that it was probably a good thing that the wood was so noisy – because it would muffle their footsteps. 'If there are others on this island, like I suspect,' he added, 'it's better that they don't hear us!' They were just passing the next tree when Timmy suddenly started jumping at it. Someone had carved a message into the bark! When they tried to read it, however, they realised it had been written in code. 'It's a good job we have codebooks with us,' remarked Julian as they eagerly started to look for them.

*Use your **CODEBOOK CARD** to find out what the message said by decoding the instruction below. If you don't have one, go to 5 instead.*

98

They had nearly pulled Dick to the top again when Julian suddenly let go of the winch's handle. It was beginning to blister his hands and he couldn't hold it a moment longer! Fortunately, the girls were able to stop the handle spinning back too far but not before Dick had slipped nearly all the way to the bottom. When they had finally pulled Dick all the way up again, they were surprised to see that he had the rucksack with him. 'I won't need the torch after all,' he said with a smile, 'I suddenly felt the rucksack right next to where I ended up!' To celebrate the safe return of both Dick and the rucksack, they decided to have some of their picnic before continuing on their way.

*Take one **PICNIC CARD** from your **LUNCHBOX**. Now go to 56.*

99

Making their way through the trees again, they expected to arrive at the castle at any moment now. Suddenly, though, Timmy stopped, pricking up his ears. 'What is it, Timmy?' George asked tensely but then she heard it herself – the faint sound of someone humming. They all quickly hid behind the nearest tree as the humming came nearer. But then Timmy suddenly ran out and the children could hear him giving the person a friendly lick! 'Why, it's Wilfrid!' they all exclaimed, as they at last dared to have a look. Biting into the sandwich Dick offered him, Wilfrid said that he had decided to come to the island after all and that he had been humming to keep up his courage!

Take one PICNIC CARD from your LUNCHBOX. Now go to 309. (Remember: when there are no picnic cards left in your lunchbox, the game has to stop and you must start all over again.)

100

While they were still deciding who should climb first up the steps, Anne noticed a scrap of paper on the dungeon floor. 'It must have dropped out of one of the men's pockets,' she said as she picked it up. They saw that there was a message on it and they held it nearer to the burning torch in the wall to see what it said. *FOR QUICKEST ROUTE TO CAVE*, it began . . . but the rest was in code. They hurriedly looked through their rucksacks for their codebooks!

Use your CODEBOOK CARD to find out what the message

said by decoding the instruction below. If you don't have one, go to 293 instead.

101

They were just about to take their maps out when Wilfrid gave a sudden shriek. 'Look, jellyfish,' he yelled in horror as he pointed all around them, 'hundreds and hundreds of them!' The others looked up too. No one had noticed them before but Wilfrid was right – they were all over the beach! They suddenly decided they didn't want to stay there a moment longer and ran for the cave. On the way, Anne's lunchbox sprang open and some of her sandwiches fell out. They dropped right in the middle of two big, ugly jellyfish and so, much too scared to pick them up, she just left them there!

Take one PICNIC CARD from your LUNCHBOX. Now go to 225.

102

As they were taking their compasses out, Dick suddenly dropped his on the floor. It made a loud tinkling sound all round the cavern. They all froze to the spot, expecting the men to rush in on them. Fortunately, it looked as if they hadn't heard anything, though, and Dick guiltily picked up his compass again! **Go to 299.**

'Let's have a quick rest,' panted George, as they had been hurrying through the wood for a good half hour now, 'I feel as if I'm about to collapse!' Although Julian was anxious to get back to the boat he agreed, since he thought there was no point in arriving there puffed out with all that rowing to be done. As soon as she had sat down, George immediately took a long gulp of her ginger beer!

Take one PICNIC CARD from your LUNCHBOX. Now go to 60.

Before anyone had found their torch, however, they heard a loud crash from down the passage . . . followed by a long moaning sound. The man had obviously tripped and hurt himself! They therefore decided that there was time to climb the rope after all. The last to go up was Julian – carrying Timmy in his rucksack! 'Hey, guess what this shaft is?' the others asked him as they helped him out, 'it's the well where we stopped before!' After pulling the rope up so the man couldn't follow them, they hurriedly set off towards where they had hidden their boat. Dick threw out some of his sandwiches on the way to make his lunchbox lighter.

Take one PICNIC CARD from your LUNCHBOX. Now go to 12.

105

Julian's compass was so difficult to read in the dark, however, that the coastguard offered to take them to the police station himself. 'If it is as urgent as you say,' he remarked on the way, 'you don't want to risk getting lost!' It wasn't long before he was pointing out the station's little blue light in the distance. 'There it is!' he said. 'Perhaps you could make your own way from now on because I have other business to see to.' Before he left, however, George gave him a large slice of her cake to show how grateful they were. 'That's most kind, most kind,' he said. 'I'll have it for my tea!'

Take one PICNIC CARD from your LUNCHBOX. Now go to 119. (Remember: when there are no picnic cards left in your lunchbox, the game is over and you must start again.)

106

'You won't need to look at your map after all,' Julian told George excitedly as he suddenly spotted a large, dark hole in the cliffs ahead. 'Look, there the cave is!' The pilot switched off all the boat's lights as they quietly approached. 'Now all we have to do is wait,' said the sergeant when they had gone as close as they dared. *Go to 26.*

107

Just as they were about to open their rucksacks, however, they heard a faint engine noise in the distance. It was the gang's boat! George jumped so much that she knocked her lunchbox over the side. 'It's a good job the men didn't hear it!' she remarked as she ducked down with the others.

Take one PICNIC CARD from your LUNCHBOX. Now go to 51.

It was Dick who picked the longest blade of grass and he led them towards a little telescope at the cliff edge. 'This can't be the right way down to the beach,' said George, 'we seem to be climbing higher rather than lower.' But Dick explained that the telescope would enable them to see where the beach was and work out a good route. He put in a coin, moving the telescope round. By the time he had spotted the beach, however, the money ran out and the telescope suddenly went dark. It was the only coin they had! 'We'll just have to use our maps to find the way,' said Julian. 'Let's hope they show the telescope, then we'll know exactly where we are.'

Do you have a MAP in your RUCKSACK? If so, use it to find out which square the telescope is in – then follow the instruction. (Remember to put the CARD back in your RUCKSACK afterwards.) If you don't have a MAP CARD, you'll have to guess which instruction to follow.

If you think E4	go to 66
If you think E2	go to 184
If you think E3	go to 218

As they were taking their codebooks out, however, Timmy started to give a frantic bark. The boat was being drawn nearer and nearer to the cliffs by a strong current! Julian and Dick started to pull on the oars for all they were worth, desperately trying to move into calmer water again. Finally, they managed it – but the message had once more become too small to read. 'Oh well, it wasn't worth getting smashed to pieces for,' said Dick with a sigh. *Go to 176.*

110

Dick said that at high tide the cave might fill with water, though, and their boat could be washed away. So they decided not to investigate it after all. Before they looked for somewhere else to hide their boat, they all agreed to have some of their picnic. The journey there had been such hard work that they felt absolutely famished. 'I could eat a horse!' said George as she opened her lunchbox. Timmy slightly backed away from her as she said this. If she could eat a horse, he seemed to be thinking, maybe she could eat a dog too! 'Oh, don't be silly, Timmy!' George laughed, handing him a sandwich. 'It's just an expression!'

Take one PICNIC CARD from your LUNCHBOX. Now go to 82.

111

Following their compasses, they counted out the 70 paces, finally reaching an iron grid across the ground. Underneath was a dark stairway that twisted deep into the earth. 'This must be it!' Wilfrid cried as they all helped lift the rusty grid up. *Go to 201.*

112

Finally agreeing that Dick's suggestion sounded best, they all followed him towards the tall tower. 'I know if I had treasures to hide,' he said as he led the way up the narrow, crumbling steps, 'I would choose right at the top of here!' When they finally reached the top of the tower, however, they saw that the only things there were a few old cauldrons. 'They were probably for pouring oil on to people who tried to attack the castle,' said Julian. As he was speaking, he suddenly noticed an iron grid covering a small hole in the ground way, way below. They decided to return to the bottom again to investigate. Just before leaving, though, George had the idea of looking up a not-too-distant creek on their maps so they would know which part of the island this was.

Use your MAP CARD to find which square the creek (a narrow inlet in the cliffs) is in – then follow the instruction. If you don't have one, you'll have to guess which instruction to follow.

If you think A1	go to 268
If you think C1	go to 139
If you think B1	go to 126

113

'Look, a tree-house!' Dick suddenly exclaimed as they continued to press ahead. He was pointing to a little wooden hut high up in the branches. 'It looks more like an observation hut,' said Julian as they walked round the bottom of the long ladder that led up to it. Thinking that they might be able to see the castle from up there, they decided to climb the ladder. 'Yes, there it is,' shouted Julian when they were all crowded into the little hut, '– about half a mile over there!' So they would know which direction to go when they were back at the bottom again, Anne had the bright idea of checking it on their compasses.

Use your COMPASS CARD to find the castle's direction by placing exactly over the shape below – and with pointer touching

north. Then go to the number that appears in the window. If you don't have one, you'll have to guess which of the numbers to go to.

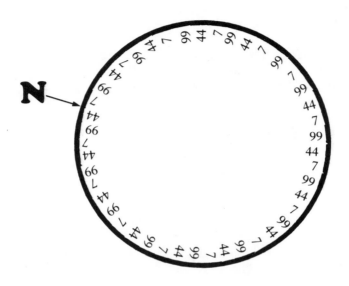

114

Just as they were about to use their compasses however, George gave a concerned cry. 'Where's Timmy?' she asked anxiously. 'He's suddenly disappeared!' Worried that he might have fallen down a pot-hole or something, they all started looking for him. 'Oh, where is he?' George wailed. 'I can't see him anywhere!' Suddenly, though, they heard a bark from the very back of the cave and they hurried over to it. Timmy was as right as rain, standing with a smile all over his face at the start of the tunnel! 'Clever boy, Timmy!' the others cheered but all George was concerned about was that she had found him again. And just to prove it, she gave him a large piece of her cake as they set off along the tunnel!

Take one PICNIC CARD from your LUNCHBOX. Now go to 262.

115

The coded message said that the cave was two miles further along. 'But two miles which way?' wondered George. 'Going clockwise round the island or anti-clockwise?' It certainly was a problem. If they chose the wrong way round, they might well end up walking much further than they need! 'We'll just have to hope for the best,' said Julian as he tossed a coin for it. The coin came down 'heads' and so they went in a clockwise direction. *Go to 9.*

116

The coded message said that the crates were to be kept firmly closed so that no one would realise what was inside. This made them curious but they decided they must give priority to finding the passage. 'We can come back and investigate the crates later,' said Julian as he led the way towards the cave. *Go to 225.*

117

Julian decided he had better do the steering himself to begin with to make sure they missed all the rocks around the island. They hadn't rowed out far when Anne suddenly noticed something very strange on top of the cliffs. It was a number of gigantic letters made out of bracken and sticks! They wondered what they were for but then Dick suddenly realised. 'It must be a coded message to tell the gang's boat where to land,' he said excitedly. 'They're probably going to set it alight so that it can be seen in the dark!' He then suggested they should take out their codebooks to find out what the message said.

*Find out as well by using your **CODEBOOK CARD** to decode the instruction below. If you don't have one, go to 294 instead.*

118

Having found the golf course on their maps, they then made their way up the cliffs towards it. Fortunately, there was a series of little wooden steps nearby built into the rock. 'I wonder which way we go now?' asked Julian when they at last arrived at the golf course. 'We had better find out soon because it seems to be getting darker by the second!' *Go to 25.*

119

Arriving at the police station, they all hurried up to the sergeant's desk. Julian quickly told him about the gang on the island and how a boat was going to come and collect both them and the treasures that very night. 'Well, it's all happening today,' the sergeant said as he immediately summoned together all his men, 'we've just heard that

Major Bullen has disappeared from the golf club with every penny of its funds!' The police took The Five with them down to the beach, helping them aboard a special police patrol boat. 'Now I would like you to do your best to direct us to this cave,' said the sergeant as he switched on the engine. 'Who's going to point the way?'

Throw the FAMOUS FIVE DICE to decide.

JULIAN thrown	go to 257
DICK thrown	go to 38
GEORGE thrown	go to 146
ANNE thrown	go to 14
TIMMY thrown	go to 182
MYSTERY thrown	go to 207

120

While they were feeling for a torch, George accidentally knocked her lunchbox and it crashed against the deck. When she opened it, she found that her bottle of ginger beer had broken! Luckily, the men didn't seem to hear the crash but the sergeant said they had better forget about looking for their torches in case any further noise was made.

Take one PICNIC CARD from your LUNCHBOX. Now go to 51.

121

Timmy was left with the longest blade of grass and so they let him run ahead while they all followed. They were just thinking they should be arriving at the beach soon when Julian spotted a little yellow flag ahead. They were back at the golf course! To begin with, they worried that something had gone wrong with Timmy's sense of direction but then they saw him start to dig in some of the rough. Not long after he had brought out a bone! 'Naughty Timmy,' George scolded, 'you've brought us all this way just because you remember sniffing a bone last time you were here.' This time, they decided, they would use their maps to find the beach! They took them out from their rucksacks, looking up the golf course so they would know where they were.

Do you have a MAP in your RUCKSACK? If so, use it to find out which square the golf course is in – then follow the instruction. (Remember to put the CARD back in your RUCKSACK afterwards.) If you don't have a MAP CARD, you'll have to guess which instruction to follow.

<blockquote>
If you think C4   go to 94
If you think D4   go to 148
If you think E4   go to 15
</blockquote>

<blockquote>
122
</blockquote>

At first, Julian wasn't sure it was a good idea to let Timmy steer but then he noticed he was rather clever at it. With the steering rope in his teeth, he would jerk his head to one side to make the boat turn right and to the other side to make it turn left! Timmy had been steering them like this for quite a way when Anne suddenly thought she saw a light flash from the island. They all waited to see if it would flash again but nothing happened. 'Perhaps they're waiting for someone to signal back from the mainland,' suggested Julian – and then he suddenly had an idea! They could use one of their torches to pretend to send a reply and the light might be tricked into flashing again. If it did, then it would prove that the island was still inhabited!

Use your TORCH to try out this idea by placing exactly over the shape below – then follow the instruction to see what happens. If you don't have a TORCH CARD in your RUCKSACK, go to 53 instead.

123

Their torches switched on, they cautiously stepped inside the cave. 'Ooh, it's a bit scary,' said Anne, her voice echoing round the walls, 'let's find somewhere else to hide the boat.' Julian eventually agreed. Not so much for Anne's reason, though, but because he was worried that at high tide the cave might fill with water and the boat would be washed away. Just as they were returning to the entrance, Dick noticed a sheet of paper wedged into the cave's damp wall. 'Look, it's a map of the island!' he exclaimed. 'Let's take it with us in case it has more on it than ours.'

If you don't already have it, put the MAP CARD into your RUCKSACK. Now go to 82.

124

Some time after leaving the graveyard, Anne tripped on a sprawling tree-root and dropped the contents of her rucksack all over the path. The others helped her pick everything up but George noticed that her torch was missing. 'It must have fallen out while I was looking for my map back at the graveyard,' Anne tutted. Dick asked whether they should go back for it but Julian said it was too far and they would just have to leave it.

If you have it, remove the TORCH CARD from your RUCK-SACK. Now go to 188.

125

'Perhaps no one need go down after all,' said Julian, suddenly noticing a large iron hook in the grass, '– we could try and grab hold of the rucksack with *this*!' So they quickly tied the hook on to the end of the rope and lowered it down. It was so dark inside the well, however, that they didn't know whether they were moving the hook in the right direction. 'I know,' exclaimed George after several minutes without success, 'let's shine our torches down. It should be a lot easier then!'

Use your TORCH CARD to light the well up by placing exactly over the shape below – then follow the instruction. If you don't have one, go to 70 instead.

```
A  G   FS    O  B E Z  T    R C    T    F D  O
  @   Z   J S  O K £  N    E  L F      M £ T
    F  N P   I    O N  £ Q K U V    R      E
  R  N  T   I  H £ O  R    N   E PN    E L
```

As soon as they had found the creek on their maps, they hurried back down the stairs, rushing over to the grid Julian had seen. 'It must be the entrance to the dungeons!' Wilfrid said excitedly as they discovered a stone stairway underneath. What was more, someone else must have come this way recently – for, part of the way down, Anne spotted a codebook on one of the steps!

If you don't already have it, put the CODEBOOK CARD into your RUCKSACK. Now go to 201.

'The cliffs are due east from here,' Julian told the others when he had reached the bottom of the folly again. 'So all we have to do is keep following east on our compasses!' It wasn't long now before they arrived at the cliff-top and they decided to follow it round until they spotted the cave. They all walked along briskly, thinking how nice it was to feel the sun on them again. *Go to 46.*

They all followed Timmy into the heart of the cave, staying as close behind him as possible. 'I do hope there aren't any hidden pot-holes,' said Wilfrid. The others had their worries too – even Timmy! His worry was that there might be some crabs lurking around the cave floor and they would pinch his paws! But without any disaster they reached the back of the cave and soon found the narrow opening that was the start of the tunnel. The tunnel became darker and darker as they followed it along and so George suggested they should take out one of their torches.

Use your TORCH CARD to light up the way by placing exactly over the shape below – then follow the instruction. If you don't have one, go to 22 instead.

```
S  G    V  E  O  ! H T    Z  R  H  T  R E    O
  Q  E    T    O    W    S      M    YN  R  O   E T
E F    N C    I    E N Z T @ H    V    E S      E
  T  S  F    E    O    O    U    N    R    Z E      ! D
```

129

Their maps showed several caves but it was easy to tell which this was on the map because it was the one right next to a series of steps. They decided the men had now had ample time to get clear and so they started towards the cave. Just before they reached it, however, Timmy noticed something made of red plastic sticking a fraction above the sand. He dug around it with his paws, soon pulling the object free. 'Why, it's someone's torch!' George exclaimed as she took it from him. There was something even more remarkable – when she pressed the torch's switch, she found that it worked just as good as new! Knowing how useful a spare torch might be in the cave, they took it with them.

If you don't already have it, put the TORCH CARD into your RUCKSACK. Now go to 225.

130

The coded message said that the treasures were to be taken to France and sold on the illegal market. 'This diary obviously belongs to one of those men,' said Julian, putting it in his rucksack as evidence for the police. They were just about to set off again when Wilfrid noticed something else lying on the ground. It was a torch! 'I dare say this belongs to them as well,' Julian added. 'But we could do with a spare – and so I think we'll make it ours!'

If you don't already have it, put the TORCH CARD into your RUCKSACK. Now go to 60.

131

Before they had agreed who was to go first up the rope, however, they suddenly heard a voice from further back down the passage. 'It's that man who locked us in,' said Dick with alarm, '– he must have heard us escape!' They wondered how near he was and if they would all have time to climb up the rope. They didn't want one person still left there and having to tackle the man on his own! Then Anne suddenly had an idea. They could shine a torch up the passage and see if he was visible yet. If he wasn't, then there was probably still time for them all to climb out. If he was, then they would all stay and deal with him together. With every second vital, therefore, they started to feel for their torches!

Use your TORCH CARD to light up the passage by placing exactly over the shape below – then follow the instruction. If you don't have one, go to 104 instead.

```
X G B   T O S   R   E   O A   T   E O   O
  Z T T  O A   *O   W   O N I    £  E
T   Y E    S I £ O Y K G H    X    T Z    B
A   F T    I  H I  !  R   V   E   R D E   A
```

132
'It's a good job your compass shines in the dark!' Dick said to Julian as they followed its direction. Breaking into a trot every so often, they were soon able to see the police station's tiny blue light in the distance. 'I just hope we're not too late!' said Anne as they hurried towards it. *Go to 119.*

133
They were now within a few hundred metres of the cave and the sergeant ordered the pilot to dim the lights and switch off the engine. 'We'll wait here until there's some sign of action,' he told the children tensely. So they all peered across the water at the cave's dark, silent entrance, hoping the gang hadn't already left. *Go to 93.*

134

While he was searching through his rucksack, however, Julian accidentally knocked his lunchbox and it toppled over the edge into the water. They all held their breath in case the splash attracted the gang's attention. Fortunately, it didn't but the sergeant said they had better forget looking through their rucksacks so they didn't risk any further noise.

Take one PICNIC CARD from your LUNCHBOX. Now go to 51.

135

The longest piece of grass was drawn by George and so they all agreed on her idea, following her back towards the golf course. 'We'll find Lucas again,' she said, 'and ask him to direct us.' Lucas was busy looking for lost golf balls, popping them into a bucket. 'Hello again,' said George, 'we wondered if you could tell us the way to the beach?' Lucas put the bucket on the ground before answering. 'Well, let me see,' he said slowly, 'you must go to hole number 8 and then walk south-west for a hundred metres. That will bring you to a little path that climbs all the way down.' When they reached hole number 8, they all searched through their rucksacks for their compasses.

Do you have a COMPASS in your RUCKSACK? If so, use it to find the right direction by placing exactly over the shape below – and with pointer touching north. Then go to the number that appears in the window. (Remember to put the CARD back in your RUCKSACK afterwards.) If you don't have a COMPASS CARD, you'll have to guess which of the numbers to go to.

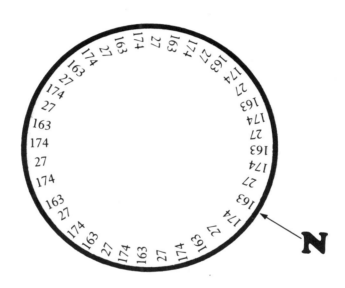

136

The message on the tree said that the treasures had been *seen* but they were well protected by fierce guards! They wondered who could have written this but then George suddenly realised. 'It must have been one of those men from the London museum,' she said. 'He must have written it so others would know in case the guards killed him.' A lot more excited now that they knew the treasures were still there, they began to row much faster! *Go to 176.*

137

The writing on the wood worked out as someone's name – *DR. PHILIP HARGREAVES*. They all wondered who he was but then Dick suddenly remembered where he had heard that name before. He was one of the museum men who had gone missing on the island! 'Perhaps he was taken captive,' Dick added, 'and he secretly wrote his name on the wood so that others might come looking for him.' They were still thinking about this when George noticed that the cliffs dropped down to a small sandy beach on the left of the island. 'That will be a good place to land,' she said as they started to row towards it. *Go to 82.*

138

Timmy began yapping excitedly, showing that he wanted to be the one to go down. 'Oh, don't be so silly, Timmy,' Dick told him, 'how could you possibly hang on to the rope?' Timmy suddenly started digging amongst some nearby bushes, though, finally bringing out an old bucket. 'Look, it must be the bucket for the well,' George exclaimed, tying it to the end of the rope, '– and Timmy's suggesting that he should sit inside!' Letting him have his wish, they carefully lowered him down. Not long after, they were bringing him up again – and with Anne's rucksack in his mouth! In the middle of patting him on the head, George noticed that the bucket had a coded message scratched on to the bottom. They quickly searched for their codebooks!

*Use your **CODEBOOK CARD** to find out what the message said by decoding the instruction below. If you don't have one, go to 283 instead.*

The others said they could look it up on their maps later – they were anxious to find the treasures first! They hurried back down the steps, rushing over to the iron grid they had seen from the top. Lifting it up, they discovered a narrow stone staircase underneath, twisting deep down into the ground. 'It must lead to the dungeons!' Julian said excitedly as he cautiously led the way in. He wasn't cautious enough, though, because part of the way down he missed a step and the rucksack slipped off his back as he stumbled. Luckily, he was all right but none of them noticed that his codebook had fallen out!

*If you have it, remove the **CODEBOOK CARD** from your **RUCKSACK**. Now go to 201.*

The coded message was taking so long to work out, however, that they decided just to leave it and concentrate on finding that cave. 'I hope it's not on the other side of the island,' said Wilfrid as they started to follow the cliff edge round, 'or it's going to take all day!' The salty air soon made them all quite thirsty and so they decided to stop for a moment to have some of their ginger beer. 'Mmm, delicious!' said Wilfrid, as Anne kindly shared her bottle with him.

Take one PICNIC CARD from your LUNCHBOX. Now go to 9.

Having followed Timmy to the bottom of the steps, they decided to sit down for a moment on the narrow stretch of sand. They pretended it was for a quick rest but the real reason was to put off entering that forbidding cave for as long as possible! Peering across the sea, they could just make out the mainland in the distance. 'Look, there's Wilfrid's cottage!' George exclaimed on spotting a tiny white shape high above the cliffs. She then suggested looking up the cottage on their maps so they would know roughly where the cave was opposite.

Use your MAP CARD to find which square the cottage is in – then follow the instruction. If you don't have one, you'll have to guess which instruction to follow.

If you think E2	go to 101
If you think E3	go to 88
If you think E4	go to 192

The tunnel finally widened into a large underground cavern. But it didn't seem to have any way out! 'I don't understand it,' said Julian, scratching his head, 'those men can't have just disappeared, surely?' Just at that moment, though, they heard their voices from behind the rock somewhere. There must be some sort of secret exit! They tried to work out from which part exactly the voices were coming but there was such an echo in the cavern that it made it impossible. But then they heard one of the men telling the others how to find the hidden exit when he wasn't there with them. He said that it was at the south side of the cavern. The Five quickly looked for their compasses!

Use your COMPASS CARD to find where south is by placing exactly over the shape below – and with pointer touching north. Then go to the number that appears in the window. If you don't have one, you'll have to guess which of the numbers to go to.

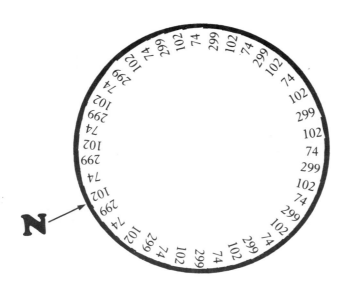

143

'Stop where you are!' the man ordered, and he made the children sit down on the dungeon floor. 'You're lucky we don't throw you from the cliffs like those two snoopers from the museum,' he added, '– but, instead, we'll keep you in here until the operation's over.' At that, he put a key to the door from the tunnel and locked it. And, when he had gone back up the steps, they could hear him standing guard at the top! 'He's blocked every exit,' George exclaimed with alarm, 'there's absolutely no way out! *Go to 315.*

144

Anne's idea was to wait until they had got back up the cliffs and then search for something they could look up on their maps. Luckily, they had no trouble in finding a way up – a series of narrow wooden steps set into the rock – but the top seemed to be completely empty of landmarks. Finally, though, they came across a small monument – consisting of an anchor leaning against a rock. 'Perhaps this will be shown!' said George as they hurriedly started to search for their maps.

Use your MAP CARD to find which square the anchor-monument is in – then follow the instruction. If you don't have one, you'll have to guess which instruction to follow.

If you think D4	go to 256
If you think D3	go to 295
If you think E3	go to 49

Out of breath, The Five finally reached the top of the cliff. 'Now I wonder which way we go?' asked Dick. Looking all about them, they suddenly spotted a white signpost. 'Perhaps that will say where the police station is!' George exclaimed as they ran towards it. The sky had now become so dark, however, that the letters on the signpost's arms were impossible to see. 'We'll have to use our torches,' said Julian, hurriedly slipping off his rucksack so he could take his out.

Use your TORCH CARD to help read the signpost by placing exactly over the shape below – then follow the instruction. If you don't have one, go to 92 instead.

George insisted on doing the directing so she could sit at the front with the pilot. The police boat of course was much faster than a rowing-boat and they were very soon nearing the island again. 'You keep following the cliffs round to the right,' George said as the spray leapt up at the window. She could just see an old graveyard on the cliff-tops above and she decided to look it up on her map to find out how much further they had to go.

Use your MAP CARD to find which square the old graveyard is in – then follow the instruction. If you don't have one, you'll have to guess which instruction to follow.

If you think C2	go to 106
If you think C3	go to 64
If you think C4	go to 196

147

Before The Five could quite see who was at the wheel, however, the man realised what was happening and quickly pulled in his anchor. 'Blow,' exclaimed the sergeant as the boat suddenly accelerated and managed to slip past them, 'he's got away!' Although they could have given chase, it would have meant letting the rest of the gang on the shore escape and so the sergeant decided to pick them up instead. 'We'll just have to catch their leader another time,' he consoled himself, 'I dare say he'll be back to see if there are any other treasures on the island!' And when he did come back, thought The Five, they would be around to help foil him!

Your adventure wasn't quite successful. If you would like another attempt at solving the mystery, you must start the game again from paragraph one. Try choosing a different EQUIP-MENT CARD this time to see if it gives you any more luck.

On their way to the beach, they decided to stop for a quick picnic. 'Well, you don't really deserve any,' said George, as Timmy eagerly pushed his nose into her lunchbox, 'but I suppose we would be lost without you!' Timmy gave her an affectionate lick before turning his attention to her delicious sandwiches. He promised himself that he wouldn't look for another bone all day!

Take one PICNIC CARD from your LUNCHBOX. Now go to 94.

They were still trying to decide who was to steer when a small motor-boat came up to them, gently chugging at their side. 'Hello!' said the owner, a friendly-looking man in a blazer and captain's cap, '– would you like a tow for some of the way? It's a lot easier than rowing.' Not only easier, The Five all thought together, but probably a lot more fun as well! The man gave Julian and Dick a rope to hold that he used for pulling water-skiers and carefully started to increase speed. 'Ooh, isn't this wonderful!' they all cried as the spray licked at their faces. *Go to 304.*

The decoded message said that boats should come ashore on the right side of the bay since there were traps on the left side. 'How horrid,' remarked Julian as they dragged their boat up on to the sand, 'they've obviously put the traps down deliberately so that anyone ignorant of the code would be wrecked. I suppose the people who wrote the message thought the code was only known by their friends.' Fortunately, though, the people were wrong . . . thanks to their codebooks, The Five knew it too! *Go to 54.*

151

'I've never seen such a dark wood!' said Julian as he led the way through the trees. The leaves and branches were so thick that you could barely see the sky above. The wood seemed to grow darker and darker, spookier and spookier, but eventually they spotted a large clearing in front. 'Why, it's a small lake!' exclaimed Dick when they came up to it. 'Whoever would have thought it – right in the middle of this wood!' When they had found a fallen tree trunk to rest on, Julian suggested they should look up the lake on their maps as a rough guide to where they were.

Use your MAP CARD to find which square the lake is in – then follow the instruction. If you don't have one, you'll have to guess which instruction to follow.

If you think B3	go to 209
If you think C3	go to 267
If you think D3	go to 30

152

Julian led them towards a stone doorway in the far corner of the courtyard. Passing through, they found themselves in a large, dark room. 'This must have been the castle's kitchen,' he said, noticing a huge fireplace with an iron spit still across it. There were some old cooking pots there as well. 'Perhaps the treasures were hidden in those!' Dick exclaimed, eagerly going over to them. Although he didn't find any treasures inside, he did find a scrap of paper. And on it there was scribbled a message! *FOR ENTRANCE TO DUNGEONS*, it read, *WALK 100 PACES SOUTH-EAST.* Maybe the treasures were hidden there, then! Hardly able to contain their excitement, they started looking for their compasses.

Use your COMPASS CARD to find south-east by placing exactly over the shape below – and with pointer touching north. Then go to the number that appears in the window. If you don't have one, you'll have to guess which of the numbers to go to.

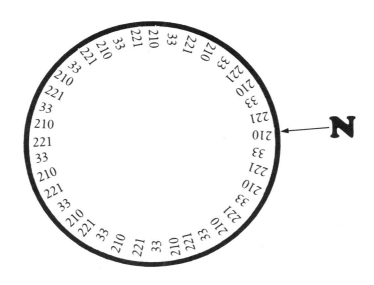

153

'Wait, there it is!' George shouted as they shone their torches down the hole. 'Move the hook just a little bit more to the right!' The rucksack was soon coming up again – a little wet but no real damage had been done. 'It was a good job the well wasn't dry,' Anne said with relief, 'or all my equipment would almost certainly have been smashed to pieces!' *Go to 113.*

The coded message said that there was a secret stairway under the floor and to find it they should look for a loose slab. 'Here it is!' cried Dick after a while as he trod on one that wobbled slightly. Lifting the slab up, they discovered some narrow stone steps that twisted deep into the ground. 'They must go down to the dungeons!' said Julian as he excitedly led the way. *Go to 190.*

One of the men struck a match and lit an old-fashioned torch in the wall only a metre or so away from them. The Five then heard them say something about meeting at the cave for the night-time loading. Fortunately, the men had soon gone again and the children all came out from their hiding place. 'There's obviously something bad going on here,' Julian said seriously. 'I suggest we creep out and try and find this cave.' So when they had given the men time to get clear, they prepared to climb the dark steps again.

Throw the FAMOUS FIVE DICE to see who is to go first.

JULIAN thrown	go to 285
DICK thrown	go to 32
GEORGE thrown	go to 253
ANNE thrown	go to 45
TIMMY thrown	go to 222
MYSTERY thrown	go to 100

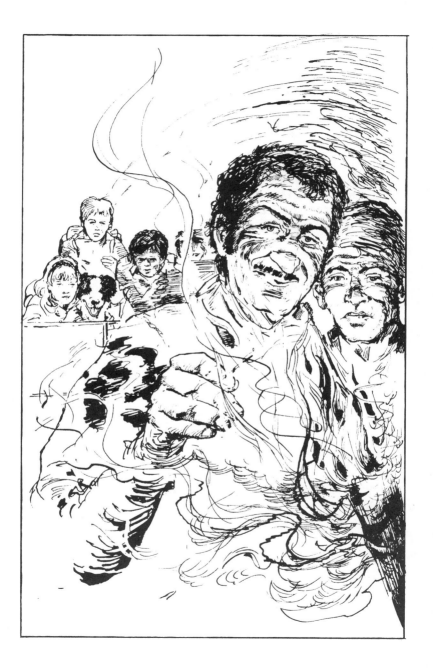

The wind howled all around them as they carefully followed Dick down the steps in the cliff. 'Be careful you don't slip,' he called back to the others, '– it's a long fall if anyone does!' About half way down, the steps widened a bit as if this was intended as a resting place. 'What a good idea,' said George, as they all sat down on the wide part, 'I was just beginning to feel dizzy!' While they were having their breather, Julian suggested they should look up the cliff steps on the map in case they needed to come this way again.

Use your MAP CARD to find which square the cliff steps are in – then follow the instruction. If you don't have one, you'll have to guess which instruction to follow.

If you think D3	go to 59
If you think D1	go to 243
If you think D4	go to 270

157

Having found south-east on their compasses, they walked the 25 paces as the message instructed. It brought them to a narrow opening right at the back of the cave. 'This is it!' cried George as they all squeezed into a long, dark tunnel. *Go to 262.*

158

Dick was right – the coded message *did* say how to find the tunnel, leading them to a narrow gap in the back wall! The tunnel was much longer than they expected, though, and they were beginning to worry that this wasn't the one the men had used after all. Maybe the message had deliberately sent them down the wrong one and they would be lost forever! Just at that moment, though, Timmy found a compass on the tunnel floor and that proved that the men *had* come this way. Indeed, it was only a few metres further that the tunnel came to an end at a large wooden door. They slowly opened it, wondering what was on the other side . . .

If you don't already have it, put the COMPASS CARD into your RUCKSACK. Now go to 245.

159

It was decided that Timmy should go up the rope first so the others could give him a hand from underneath. 'Make sure your teeth grip the rope really hard,' Julian told him as he kept giving his back-end little pushes with his head! When they all finally reached the top, they realised what the shaft was. 'Why, it's that well where we were before!' Anne exclaimed, noticing the winch. Knowing where they were now, they hurriedly set off towards where they had hidden the boat. On the way, Dick suddenly noticed a wallet on the ground. He looked inside to see who it belonged to but the owner's name was in code. 'Quick, let's look for our codebooks!' he said.

Use your CODEBOOK CARD to work out the owner's name by decoding the instruction below. If you don't have one, go to 235 instead.

160

Having found the boathouse on their maps, they then looked to see if the police station was shown as well. Unfortunately, it wasn't! 'It must be off the edge of the map,' said Julian disappointedly. Noticing it becoming darker by the second, they wondered how they were going to find the police station now! *Go to 25.*

161

'Here it is,' exclaimed Anne when she had found the pay-telescope on her map, 'about a mile further up the coast!' Running most of the way, they soon reached it but there didn't seem to be a police station in sight. 'It must be because it's so dark,' said Dick – but then he suddenly had an idea. They could see if the telescope made it any clearer! Borrowing a five-pence piece from Wilfrid, Dick slowly moved the telescope round. 'Yes, it's straight ahead!' he exclaimed, suddenly focusing on the station's tiny blue light. *Go to 119.*

162

Julian was just taking his torch out when the boat's light suddenly came on again. 'How odd,' remarked the sergeant, 'perhaps we won't need your torch after all!' The light was actually a lot dimmer than before but the sergeant said that it was probably a good thing – so their boat was harder to spot. 'We don't want to give the game away, do we!' he remarked as George offered round her ginger beer.

Take one PICNIC CARD from your LUNCHBOX. Now go to 265.

163

They must have read their compasses wrongly, though, because they seemed to be walking further and further inland. 'Oh, aren't we chumps,' exclaimed Julian suddenly, 'we set the *short* end of the pointer at north instead of the long end!' Before they returned all the way they had come, they decided to have some of their picnic to make their lunchboxes a little lighter. 'The trouble is,' joked Dick, 'it will make our tummies a little heavier!'

Take one PICNIC CARD from your LUNCHBOX. Now go to 94.

164

With Timmy proudly watching her, George steered the boat towards the west side of the island. The rowing was done by Julian and Dick together – Julian working the left oar while Dick worked the right. It wasn't long, though, before a thick mist surrounded them. 'We had better stop rowing until it clears,' advised Julian. Dick was just about to lift his oar from the water when he noticed an old bottle floating by. 'Look, there's a message in it,' he exclaimed when he had fished it out. They soon discovered that the message was in code, however, and their only chance of working it out was by using their codebooks. 'It's a good job Wilfrid lent each of us one,' said George as they began to look for them in their rucksacks.

Do you have a CODEBOOK in your RUCKSACK? If so use it to find out what the message said by decoding the instruction below. If you don't have one, go to 16 instead.

Julian carefully rowed them through the grotto's opening, reaching a large cave on the other side. 'Ooh, isn't it spooky?' said Anne, flashing her torch round the wet rock. But when they had rowed in a little further, something extraordinary happened! The water suddenly seemed to light up a bright blue colour and it was no longer spooky at all but very beautiful. 'It's the effect of the light squeezing through the small opening,' Julian explained, '– and I think the type of rock has something to do with it.' When they'd had a good look round, Julian rowed them out into the sea again and continued towards the bay that George had spotted. *Go to 176.*

Timmy insisted that he should go first in case there was any danger! The others followed closely behind as he led the way through the dark trees. Timmy cocked his head to right and left listening out for anything sinister – although Anne did secretly wonder whether it was just as much rabbits he was listening for! The trees became denser and denser, darker and darker and it was becoming quite difficult to see. 'Perhaps we should use our torches,' suggested George as she slipped off her rucksack to take hers out.

Use your TORCH as well by placing exactly over the shape below – then follow the instruction. If you don't have a TORCH CARD in your RUCKSACK, go to 290 instead.

```
E G   T H   O   £ G V   A   N £ R   T   N T   O
T   H   B R   O D !   N   E   P E   V I
N   V F   I   O V 3   U !   F   N   Z R   E
W   F N   Z @   @ S   I   V   N   Z X   E   Y
```

167

'There seems to be nothing up there but an old nest,' said Julian as he shone his torch high into the branches. Disappointed, they wondered why anyone should want to point arrows at a nest but then Dick suddenly had a brainwave. 'Perhaps there's something inside!' he exclaimed, immediately starting to climb the tree. He was soon at the level of the nest and, being careful not to dislodge it in case birds were still using it, he quietly peered in. The birds had deserted it long ago but in the middle was a small compass. He was right, someone had hidden something inside! And just in case they needed a spare, he decided to take it with him!

If you don't already have it, put the COMPASS CARD into your RUCKSACK. Now go to 30.

168

Their maps showed that the outcrop of rock was quite a bit north of the cave and so they still had some way to go. They had only gone a few steps further along the cliff-top when George suddenly noticed something catch the sunlight in the grass. 'Look, a compass, ' she exclaimed, picking it up. 'One of those men must have dropped it!' She gave it to Wilfrid so that he now had one as well.

If you don't already have it, put the COMPASS CARD into your rucksack. Now go to 46.

They were just about to use their compasses when they heard a noise right behind them. When they nervously turned round, however, there was no one there! 'The place is haunted,' cried Anne, 'quick—let's get out of here!' At that very moment, though, the voice came again and Julian realised it was just an echo from somewhere much further off. 'Of course,' he added suddenly, 'it's from those men in the tunnel! The next time it comes, let's follow its direction.' So that's what they did, tracing the sound to a narrow hole at the very back of the cave. They were so pleased at having found the start of the tunnel that they all had a quick bite of their cake to celebrate before entering.

Take one PICNIC CARD from your LUNCHBOX. Now go to 262.

Dick said he would do the steering while Julian did the rowing. Then when Julian got tired they would swap round. 'Okay,' Julian agreed, taking hold of the oars. Dick tried to think which way he would have to steer and then he remembered that to get to this part they had gone roughly north. So to find their way back again they would have to go roughly south! The girls quickly looked through the rucksacks to find him a compass.

Use your COMPASS CARD to find south by placing exactly

over the shape below – and with pointer touching north. Then go to the number that appears in the window. If you don't have one, you'll have to guess which of the numbers to go to.

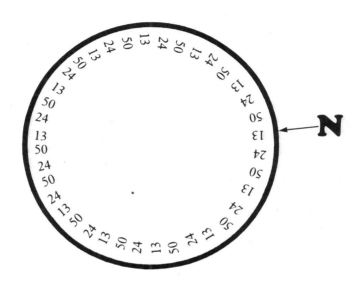

171
'Yes, there are the steps!' Dick exclaimed when they had followed their compasses to where the cliffs were less steep. They all climbed the steps two at a time, aware that it was becoming darker by the second. 'I wish I was Timmy,' puffed George as she watched him leap further and further ahead, 'he makes it look so easy!' ***Go to 145.***

172
Just as Anne was taking out her map, a gust of wind came up and snatched it out of her hand. 'Oh, no,' she cried, 'it's being blown towards the sea!' Luckily, Dick was just able to stop it in time with his foot. 'Now let's go back to looking up that golf course,' he laughed, as he handed it back to her. ***Go to 205.***

'We're travelling in a north-west direction,' the children told the sergeant when they had studied their compass. The sergeant wrote it down in a little notebook so he would remember. The cave was growing a lot nearer now and the pilot dimmed the boat's lights and reduced its speed. He soon switched the engine off altogether and they all peered across the dark silent water, waiting for the gang to appear. *Go to 93.*

'We must have read our compass wrongly,' said Julian, when they couldn't find the path down to the beach, 'we've surely walked a hundred metres by now.' So they returned all the way to hole number 8 to try again. When they were back at the yellow flag, however, Anne suddenly realised their mistake. 'Look, it's not number 8 at all,' she exclaimed, 'but number 18! The 1 is so faint that we didn't see it.' They were so hot by the time they had found the real number 8 that they decided to have a quick drink of their ginger beer before going any further.

Take one PICNIC CARD from your LUNCHBOX. Now go to 66.

Just as they were returning with their compasses, however, a large wave came in and washed the message away. What was worse, they forget what the message said! They couldn't remember whether it said walk 14 or 15 paces and whether it was north-east or south-east. Or was it south-west?! It would take all day if they tried every possibility and so they decided they would just have to leave it. What a pity – they were all beginning to find this rather exciting! *Go to 54.*

They still had some distance to go to the sandy part when a thick mist began to descend over the sea. 'I don't think we're going to reach the bay in time,' said Julian anxiously, knowing that once the mist surrounded them they wouldn't be able to see which way to steer. They were all just starting to panic when Anne had a clever idea. They could check the bay's direction on their compasses before it disappeared and then they would know which way to steer even with the mist! So they quickly searched for their compasses while there was still time.

Do you have a COMPASS in your RUCKSACK? If so, use it to check the bay's direction by placing exactly over the shape below – and with pointer touching north. Then go to the number that appears in the window. If you don't have a COMPASS CARD, you'll have to guess which of the numbers to go to.

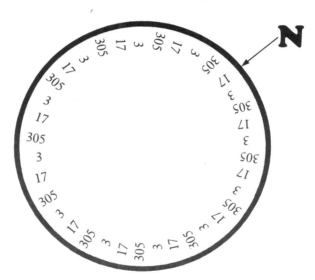

Since it was Anne who had caused the trouble, she thought it only right that she should go down. 'Besides,' she added, 'I'm a lot lighter than everyone else. So it will be a lot easier to pull me up again.' The well became blacker and blacker as the others lowered her down but Anne tried not to think about it, feeling for the rucksack. At last she reached it, and it was with great relief that she shouted to the others to pull her up again. Before they left the well, Dick suggested checking if it was shown on their maps.

Use your MAP CARD to find which square the well is in – then follow the instruction. If you don't have a MAP in your RUCKSACK, you'll have to guess which instruction to follow.

If you think B2	go to 200
If you think C2	go to 301
If you think D2	go to 291

178

They were just opening their codebooks when Timmy got under Anne's feet and she stumbled to the floor. Fortunately, she only suffered a slight graze on her hand but she fell right in the middle of the pebbles. The message was sent scattering in all directions! There was even worse news. When she checked the contents of her lunchbox, she found that her bottle of ginger beer had broken. While they were looking for somewhere safe to hide the pieces of glass, Wilfrid discovered a small opening in the rock at the far end of the cave. 'It's the start of the tunnel!' Julian exclaimed as he led the way through.

Take one PICNIC CARD from your LUNCHBOX. Now go to 262.

'That's better!' George exclaimed as their torches lit up the tunnel. As they started to follow it, they tried to work out how the tunnel had been made. 'I expect it was formed by some sort of underground stream running down to the sea,' said Julian, noticing how smooth the tunnel floor was. *Go to 142.*

'I've just found out where we are,' George shouted down to the others when she had reached the top of the rope, 'we're back at that well where we were before!' Next Anne climbed up, then Dick, then Wilfrid. Last of all went Julian – carrying Timmy in his rucksack! Now they were all safely above ground again, Julian suggested they should immediately hurry back to their boat. They remembered that they had left it on a sandy beach on the west side of the island and so they looked for their maps to work out how to get there.

Use your MAP CARD to find which square the sandy beach is in – then follow the instruction. If you don't have one, you'll have to guess which instruction to follow.

If you think A1   go to 214
If you think A2   go to 103
If you think A3   go to 11

'We're about half way,' said George, when she had found the statue on her map. They all looked at their watches, trying to work it out. If it had taken them forty minutes to reach this point, then they should be back at the mainland by about half past nine. They only hoped that it wouldn't be too late! *Go to 13.*

The children insisted that Timmy show the way, since he had the best sense of direction. 'Just follow which way his nose is pointing,' George told the police boat's pilot. To begin with, the sergeant wasn't too happy about it but, as the cave at last became visible in the distance, he realised how clever Timmy was. 'Why, he's better than a police dog!' he exclaimed. He then asked the children to find out in which direction they were travelling on their compasses so he would know for his report.

Use your COMPASS CARD to check the police boat's direction by placing exactly over the shape below – and with pointer touching north. Then go to the number that appears in the window. If you don't have one, you'll have to guess which of the numbers to go to.

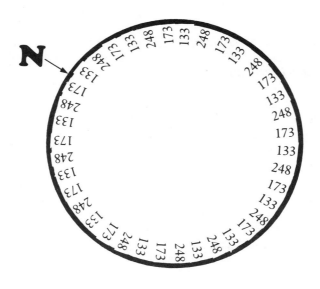

'That's better,' said the sergeant as Julian found his torch and switched it on, '– now we should be much more difficult to spot.'

The boat hadn't gone much further before George noticed something floating towards them in the water. 'It looks like some sort of notebook,' the sergeant remarked and, thinking it might have belonged to one of the gang, he put a special pole in the water to fish it out. 'It would appear that I'm right,' he said as he flicked through the waterproof pages, 'it's full of secret codes!' He asked George to look after the codebook for him until they got back to the police station.

*If you don't already have it, put the **CODEBOOK CARD** into your **RUCKSACK**. Now go to 265.*

184
Luckily, their maps *did* show the telescope and so they could see where they were. 'All we have to do is follow this path for about a mile,' said Julian, his finger pointing to a thin yellow line that started in the same square on the map. As soon as they had found the path, they put their maps away again. It was so windy at the top of the cliffs they were frightened that they might be blown away! *Go to 66.*

185
It was Julian himself who spotted somewhere, pointing to a small stretch of sand just before the next bend. 'That looks ideal,' he said eagerly. 'I was beginning to worry that it was cliffs all the way round!' Before they reached the little bay, however, Dick noticed some sort of message gouged out of the massive cliff face above them. 'Row a little closer,' he said to Julian, 'and we might be able to work out what it says.' When Julian had gone a bit nearer, though,

they realised that the message was in a secret code. 'Of course!' remarked George, just as they were about to give up and continue past, '– we can use our codebooks!'

*Use your **CODEBOOK CARD** to find out what the message said by decoding the instruction below. If you don't have a **CODEBOOK** in your **RUCKSACK**, go to 109 instead.*

186

The cliffs seemed to go all round the island, as far as the eye could see, and they were worried that they weren't going to be able to find anywhere to land. 'There must be somewhere,' said Dick, 'or how would those two men from the museum have gone ashore?' So they kept rowing round the island's coastline, waiting for a suitable place to appear. *Go to 306.*

Having found the sandy bay on their maps, Julian suggested they should mark it with a little cross so they would know where to come back for their boat. They then had a quick rest on the sand to dry out. 'Trust the wind to drop again as soon as we reach land!' Dick laughed as they watched the sea suddenly become much calmer again. *Go to 54.*

188

Some time later, they came across an old well. It was partly overgrown with weeds but the rope and bucket were still there and so they decided to try it to see if it still worked. 'Yes, it does!' they all exclaimed as they brought up some surprisingly clear water. Julian said that the well probably belonged to the owners of the castle and they must be quite close to it now. Just as they were about to set off again, however, they saw a movement between the trees. Someone was following them! *Go to 19.*

189

They followed their compasses deep into the trees again, Anne grateful that she had her rucksack safely back on her shoulders. 'It was a good job there wasn't much water in that well,' said Julian, 'or it would have been soaked through!' As they continued quietly along, Dick couldn't quite decide which he would mind losing most – his rucksack or his lunchbox! *Go to 56.*

190

The stairway finally ended at a large, dark vault. There were manacles and rusty chains set into the damp walls. 'You were right,' Anne said to Julian with a shiver, 'it *is* the dungeons!' George was examining the chains, thinking how horrid they were, when she discovered a coded message scratched into the stone. 'Perhaps it says where the treasures are hidden!' she yelled, hurriedly looking for her codebook.

*Use your **CODEBOOK CARD** to find out what the message said by decoding the instruction below. If you don't have one, go to 85.*

191

On their way along the cliff-tops, Wilfrid suddenly noticed a small pile of rocks in the grass. 'They look as if they have been stacked there deliberately as a marker or something,' he said as he ran up to them. Taking the top layer of rocks off, however, he saw that it had a different purpose! 'Hey, there's a torch underneath,' he shouted to the others, '– the rocks were obviously to shelter it.' Julian said that the torch was probably used by the men to flash signals to their partners on the mainland. Sure that there was some villainy behind the signals, he decided to thwart their schemes by taking the torch away with him!

*If you don't already have it, put the **TORCH CARD** into your **RUCKSACK**. Now go to 9.*

While they were looking for their maps, however, Anne suddenly gave an anxious shriek. The tide was coming in! It was coming in very fast too – soon within centimetres of where they were sitting. 'Quick, let's run for the cave,' said Julian, '– we can't delay it any longer!' They were in such a panic that, just before reaching the cave, George slipped on a piece of wet seaweed. She hit the beach so hard that she heard her torch shatter inside her rucksack!

If you have it, remove the TORCH CARD from your RUCK-SACK. Now go to 225.

The owner's name worked out as *EMILIO PONCHI.* 'That's obviously one of those men,' said Julian. 'They all looked rather foreign!' They decided to take the wallet with them to hand in to the police. Then if the owner wanted to go and claim it, he would have a lot of explaining to do first! **Go to 12.**

Timmy seemed to have the firmest idea where the police station was, desperately tugging at George's sleeve, and so they all followed him. He found some little wooden steps leading up the cliffs and he made them climb all the way to the top. But then his inspiration suddenly seemed to desert him and he couldn't think which way to turn. 'Never mind, Timmy,' George comforted him, 'I'm sure it's up on the cliffs somewhere.' Then she spotted the boathouse below and they decided to look it up on their maps to find out roughly where they were.

Use your MAP CARD to find which square the boathouse is in – then follow the instruction. If you don't have one, you'll have to guess which instruction to follow.

If you think A4	go to 49
If you think C4	go to 160
If you think B4	go to 295

195

On the way to the police station, George suddenly got a bad stitch! 'We shouldn't have run so fast,' said Julian, deciding to stop for a while so that she could recover. A few minutes later she was all right again but they went a lot slower this time. George also handed round some of her cake so her lunchbox was easier to carry.

Take one PICNIC CARD from your LUNCHBOX. Now go to 119.

196

By the time George had found her map, however, they had reached the cave and so she didn't need it anyway. The sergeant ordered the pilot to switch off the boat's engine and all the lights while they waited for something to happen. 'There doesn't seem to be anything yet,' Dick observed tensely as they all peered across the water at the cave's dark, silent entrance. To help pass the time, Julian offered round the remainder of his sandwiches. 'Mm, just what I need,' said the sergeant. 'You dragged me out just as I was about to have my supper!'

Take one PICNIC CARD from your LUNCHBOX. Now go to 26.

'Good boy, Timmy,' George said with a hug as he started barking at a small stretch of sand in the distance, 'I knew you would be the one to spot it first.' Before they quite reached the bay, however, they came across a red buoy bobbing up and down in the water. They were just about to steer round it when Anne noticed that there was a message written on it in white paint. 'Go in a little closer,' she told Julian, 'I can't quite see what it says.' When Julian had rowed them right up to the buoy, however, Anne realised that the message was in some sort of code. 'Perhaps our codebooks will be able to help,' said Dick, beginning to search for his in his rucksack.

Do you have a CODEBOOK in your RUCKSACK? If so, use it to find out what the message said by decoding the instruction below. If you don't have a CODEBOOK, go to 231 instead.

Anne tugged on one side of the steering rope, then the other, making the boat head for the west side of the island. 'Come on, you two,' she laughed at Julian and Dick as they did the rowing, 'put a bit more strength into it!' George laughed at them too, saying that she could go a lot faster just rowing on her own. 'It's a lot harder than it looks,' Dick retorted with a red face, 'and if you don't believe us, you jolly well *can* do the rowing on your own!' Before they got into a big argument, though, Julian suggested that George should look up the boathouse they had just left on her map. Then they would know how to get back again once they had explored the island.

Use your MAP CARD to find out which square the boathouse is in – then follow the instruction. If you don't have one you'll have to guess which instruction to follow.

If you think C4	go to 29
If you think B4	go to 281
If you think A4	go to 80

199
Their torches made the wood look even worse, however, creating weird shadows and shapes out of the trees. But if they *didn't* use their torches, they might well trip on something and hurt themselves. They only hoped that the wood soon started to thin out again! *Go to 188.*

200
They hadn't walked far from the well when some large crows started to follow them, flapping from one tree to the next. 'Ooh, they look rather unfriendly,' Anne remarked anxiously, 'I wish they would go away!' Timmy tried barking but they didn't take any notice. Suddenly, one swooped down at them, brushing Dick's lunchbox. 'They seem to be after our food,' he said, '–we'd better throw them some of our sandwiches before they start on us!' So they all took out one sandwich each, hurling them back down the path. 'It seems to have done the trick,' said Julian a little further on, when there was no more sign of the crows.

Take one PICNIC CARD from your LUNCHBOX. Now go to 113.

The stairway went down and down, seeming to twist forever. Finally, though, they reached the last step, arriving at a large dark chamber. 'Oh, those poor prisoners being kept down here!' said Anne as she shivered from the cold. They started to feel their way round the chamber, certain this was where the treasures were hidden. It was so dark, however, that they couldn't really see properly. 'Let's use our torches,' suggested George. After all, it was precisely for a situation like this that they had brought them!

Use your TORCH CARD to light up the dungeon by placing exactly over the shape below – then follow the instruction. If you don't have one, go to 310 instead.

202

The wind was so fierce at the top of the cliffs, however, that it was difficult to keep their maps open. 'We'd better forget about using them for the moment,' said George, quickly folding hers up again, 'or they'll be torn or blown away!' They had only gone a short way further when Dick suggested they should stop for some of their picnic. All this walking against the wind was making him hungry!

Take one PICNIC CARD from your LUNCHBOX. Now go to 46.

They all stuck close together as Dick led them into the heart of the cave. They could hear the steady drip of water all around them and their steps made a horrible echoing sound. There was just enough light coming through the hole for them to see and they started looking for the beginning of the tunnel. 'Hey look, what's this?' exclaimed Dick, suddenly finding a message carved into the cave wall. *FOR START OF TUNNEL*, he read the message out loud to the others, *WALK 25 PACES SOUTH-EAST*. They hurriedly searched for their compasses!

Use your COMPASS CARD to find south-east by placing exactly over the shape below – and with pointer touching north. Then go to the number that appears in the window. If you don't have one, you'll have to guess which of the numbers to go to.

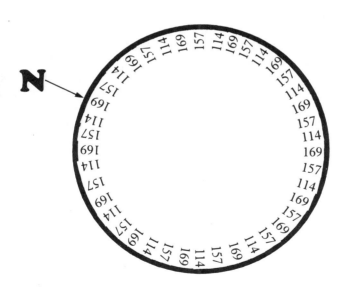

Decoding the message took so long, however, that they decided to leave it half-way through. It was much more important for them to return to the boat. Before they set off again, they quickly had some of their picnic so they wouldn't have to stop on the way.

Take one PICNIC CARD from your LUNCHBOX. Now go to 60.

Unfortunately, however, the golf course wasn't shown on their maps! 'Oh blow,' exclaimed Julian, 'it must be just off the edge!' They then asked Wilfrid if he could find the way to the golf course without a map. He said he would do his best, starting to look for a path up the cliffs first. 'I'm sure there's a series of steps just round this corner,' he told them. There *were* some steps and they hurried to the top. 'Now I think we go this way,' Wilfrid said, once they had got their breath back. Wilfrid was right again – for it wasn't long after that they spotted the golf course! 'Have some of my cake as a reward!' Dick chuckled, as he offered him the largest slice he had.

Take one PICNIC CARD from your LUNCHBOX. Now go to 25.

Just at that moment, though, the moon came out from behind a cloud and so they didn't need their torches after all. 'Don't the waves look beautiful,' remarked Anne as the moonlight tipped them with silver. Looking up, they also noticed that there were some stars appearing. 'I wonder which one is the North Star?' asked Julian and he decided to take out his compass to find out. As he was opening it, however, one of the waves gave the boat a sudden jolt and it made him drop the compass over the side. 'Oh no!' he exclaimed as he watched it quickly disappear.

If you have it, remove the COMPASS CARD from your RUCKSACK. Now go to 76.

207

None of the children were sure they could find the cave again, however, and so the sergeant radioed back to the station to see if they could help. 'H.Q. says it's probably in a north-west direction,' he told the pilot when he had got a reply and the boat was soon speeding across the water. Suddenly, though, the boat's compass seemed to go all funny and the pilot no longer knew which way to steer. 'Never mind,' said Julian, just as the sergeant was beginning to panic, 'we can find north-west on *our* compasses instead!'

Use your COMPASS CARD to find this direction by placing exactly over the shape below – and with pointer touching north. Then go to the number that appears in the window. If you don't have one, you'll have to guess which of the numbers to go to.

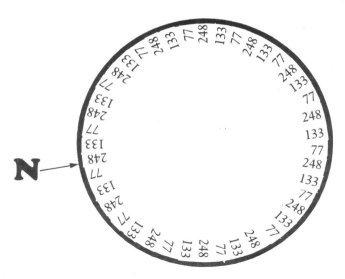

They hadn't been following their compasses far when Julian suddenly noticed something shiny in the grass. 'Look' it's a torch!' he exclaimed, picking it up, 'someone must have dropped it.' He tried the switch. It worked perfectly! 'When we return from the island,' he suggested, 'we'll hand it in at the police station. But for the moment, I'm sure the owner won't mind if we take it with us as a spare!' The others all agreed. Although they each had a torch already, an extra one might well come in useful. You could never tell on their sort of adventures!

If you don't already have it, put the TORCH CARD into your RUCKSACK. Now go to 94.

Having found the lake on their maps, they suddenly noticed that Timmy had run off somewhere. 'Look, there he is!' cried Anne, spotting him on the other side of the lake. He seemed to have picked up a scent and was following it with his nose to the ground. 'What is it, Timmy?' they all asked as they ran up to him. 'What can you smell?' He just kept sniffing the trail, though, finally stopping at an old corduroy jacket. 'I wonder if it belonged to one of those men from the museum?' Julian asked excitedly, searching for a name tag. Although he couldn't find a name, he did find a compass – it dropped from one of the pockets!

If you don't have it already, put the COMPASS CARD into your RUCKSACK. Now go to 30.

Following their compasses, they walked out into the courtyard again. Pace 90 brought them to the entrance to the tower and pace 100 to the stairway inside. One part led upwards to the top and the other twisted down into the depths below! 'The dungeons are obviously at the bottom of here!' cried Julian as he led the way. **Go to 201.**

The coded message finally worked out as: *FOR QUICKEST ROUTE TO CAVE, FOLLOW TREES WITH AN ORANGE ARROW ON THEM TO CLIFF-TOPS. THEN WALK ALONG CLIFFS IN A CLOCKWISE DIRECTION.* As soon as they had reached the wood again, therefore, they started looking for these orange arrows. They were painted on some of the tree trunks and they led all the way to the cliff-tops, just as the message had said. 'Now all we have to do is follow the cliffs round until we spot the cave,' said Julian, making sure they were pointing in a clockwise direction. On their way along the cliff edge, Dick suddenly noticed something twinkle in the short grass. It was someone's lost compass catching the sun! They decided to take it with them as a spare.

If you don't already have it, put the COMPASS CARD into your RUCKSACK. Now go to 9.

When they had followed Anne to the bottom of the steps, they decided to sit down for a while on the sand. They wanted to be sure the men had a good lead on them before they entered the cave themselves. They certainly didn't have any wish to catch them up! While they were waiting, George suggested seeing if the cave was shown on their maps. If those men were up to no good, as seemed likely, they would then be able to direct the police to it.

Use your MAP CARD to find which square the cave is in – then follow the instruction. If you don't have one, you'll have to guess which instruction to follow.

If you think D1	go to 192
If you think D3	go to 101
If you think D2	go to 129

213

'Why, it's just a crab!' Julian exclaimed with relief as his torch lit up its bright red shell. 'It must have come all the way up from the sea!' The crab quickly scampered past them and, after laughing at themselves for being so nervous, The Five continued on their way. The tunnel seemed to go on and on but, finally, it came to an end at a large wooden door. They cautiously turned the handle, wondering what was on the other side . . . *Go to 245.*

214

'I hope those men haven't found our boat and sunk it,' said Dick as they hurried on their way. But then Wilfrid reminded him that *he* had brought a boat too! Just as they were beginning to feel a lot better, though, Wilfrid had an awful thought. His boat could be on the other side of the island for all he could remember! *Go to 12.*

They were still trying to decide whose idea to follow when Dick suddenly remembered Wilfrid! 'Of course,' he exclaimed, putting a hand on his shoulder, 'we were forgetting you live round here. You're probably the best person to find the police station!' Wilfrid said that he didn't know *exactly* where it was but he did know that it was somewhere beyond the golf course. 'Okay, we'll head for the golf course!' said Dick as they all hurriedly started to look for their maps.

Use your MAP CARD to find which square the golf course is in – then follow the instruction. If you don't have one, you'll have to guess which instruction to follow.

If you think C4	go to 172
If you think D4	go to 205
If you think E4	go to 118

'I feel a lot safer now,' said Julian as he shone his torch across the dark water. Using a torch might well have other advantages too! If there were any rescue boats about, it would make it easier for the pilot to see them. 'I do hope a rescue boat does come by,' said Anne with a shiver. 'It's beginning to get quite cold.' George was beginning to feel a little cold too but it was all right for her – she could just cuddle up to Timmy! *Go to 76.*

'The cave should be just around the next bend,' George said excitedly as she found the flagpost on her map. The sergeant told the pilot to dim the boat's lights as they approached and, when they were about five hundred metres from the cave, to switch off the engine. While they were waiting for something to happen, a large gull landed on the side of the boat. 'What's that it's got in its beak?' Anne asked. To begin with, she thought it was a fish but then she realised it was some sort of small book. As the bird flew off again, it dropped the book on to the deck and Julian went to examine it. 'Why, it's a secret codebook!' he exclaimed. 'The gull must have picked it up from the beach, thinking it was food!'

If you don't already have it, put the CODEBOOK CARD into your RUCKSACK. Now go to 26.

218

It was so windy at the top of the cliffs, however, that it was impossible to keep their maps open. They were also frightened that they might be blown away. So they decided they would just have to do without them and guess the way to the beach. It must have been a good guess because it wasn't long before their path was climbing down towards a large stretch of sand below. To celebrate, they stopped for a short while to have a little of their picnic.

Take one PICNIC CARD from your LUNCHBOX. Now go to 66.

'That looks like a bay over there!' George suddenly shouted, pointing to a small patch of sand in the distance. They were rowing towards it when Julian spotted a small hole at the bottom of the cliffs. 'It looks like some sort of grotto,' he said, suggesting that they go and explore it. So they carefully rowed up to the jagged opening, peering inside. 'It's awfully dark in there,' said Dick, his voice echoing round the walls and off the water, 'we had better use our torches.'

If you have one, use your TORCH as well by placing exactly over the shape below – then follow the instruction. If you don't have a TORCH CARD in your RUCKSACK, go to 40 instead.

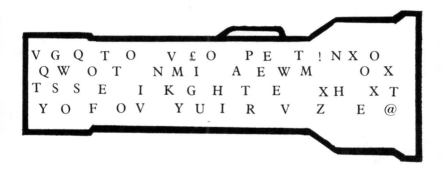

Julian said they had better save their torches for later, though, in case they couldn't get back to the boat before nightfall. Besides, they had a lot more important things to do – like finding the castle! But they all started up again a bit too quickly because Dick failed to notice a branch across the path and he tripped. Fortunately, he didn't sprain anything but when he checked his lunchbox, he found that his bottle of ginger beer had broken!

Take one PICNIC CARD from your LUNCHBOX. Now go to 30.

Timmy couldn't be bothered wasting time looking for compasses, however, going in search of the dungeons himself. His nose was just as good as any little metal pointer in a case! 'Hey, what's Timmy found?' George suddenly called to the others as she noticed him eagerly sniffing at something in the ground at the other end of the courtyard. Forgetting the search for their compasses for a moment, they hurried after him. 'Look, it's a stairway that goes deep into the ground,' Anne said, pointing to a series of steps beneath an iron grid. 'It looks like Timmy's found the dungeon entrance for us!' After Timmy had been given a big slice of George's cake as a reward, they all started to lift the grid up so they could enter the hole.

Take one PICNIC CARD from your LUNCHBOX. Now go to 201.

222

Letting Timmy go first in case those men were still hanging around, the others followed him to the top of the steps and then made a dash back into the wood. After a while, they got a glimpse of a ruined lighthouse through the trees ahead and they knew they had found the cliffs again. 'We'll just keep following them round until we spot the cave,' said Julian. Before they started, though, he suggested they should look up the lighthouse on their maps to find out which part of the coastline this was.

Use your MAP CARD to find which square the lighthouse is in – then follow the instruction. If you don't have one, you'll have to guess which instruction to follow.

If you think B1	go to 275
If you think A1	go to 191
If you think C1	go to 202

Keeping as close to the cliff-face as possible so they weren't blown over, they all followed Julian down the steps. He hadn't led them far when he noticed an empty cigarette box at his feet. 'It must have been dropped by one of those men,' he told the others over his shoulder, picking it up. When he opened the box, he saw that there was a message inside. *BOAT WILL BE COMING FROM A NORTH-EAST DIRECTION*, it read. Although they didn't know what boat it was talking about, they decided to look up north-east on their compasses in case it all made sense later on.

Use your COMPASS CARD to find north-east by placing exactly over the shape below – and with pointer touching north. Then go to the number that appears in the window. If you don't have one, you'll have to guess which number to go to.

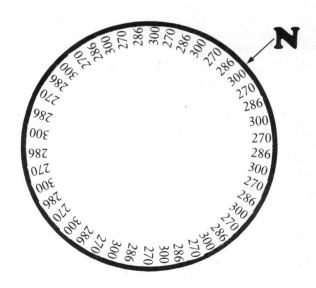

224

Just in case they needed their torches for later on, though, Dick suggested they try and do without them for the moment to save the batteries. So they all put them away again, deciding to feel along the tunnel wall instead. 'I do hope those men aren't hiding somewhere,' said Wilfrid as they peered into the darkness. To keep up their courage, they all had little sips of their ginger beer on the way.

Take one PICNIC CARD from your LUNCHBOX. Now go to 142.

225

'Ooh, I'm not sure I like it in here!' said Anne, as they passed through the cave's entrance and stood in the centre of a huge, echoing hollow. There was the steady drip of water from the cave's roof, some of it trickling down their necks. 'Let's hurry up and find this tunnel,' suggested Julian, starting to feel his way round the dark walls. Suddenly, they came across something strange. It was a coded message glowing from the rock! 'It must have been written in special paint,' exclaimed Dick, '– and I wouldn't mind betting it says where the tunnel starts!' So they hurriedly felt for their codebooks.

Use your CODEBOOK CARD to find out what the message

*said by decoding the instruction below. If you don't have one, go
to 277 instead.*

226

Julian was just about to switch on his torch when he suddenly
thought of something. Say the boat belonging to the gang came this
way and spotted them! Far from trying to avoid crashing into their
boat, they would probably do it deliberately to stop them fetching
the police! So he wisely put his torch away again, saying that if
another boat did start to come too near they would just have to
shout. 'And just to make sure our voices are clear enough,' George
added with a chuckle, 'we'd better all have some of my ginger beer!'

**Take one PICNIC CARD from your LUNCHBOX. Now go to
76.**

Dick had noticed someone collecting shell-fish further along the beach and his idea was to go and ask him. 'I've got no time to chat,' said the man as they all hurried up to him, 'I want to fill this bucket before it becomes too dark to see.' But when he heard that they were looking for the police station and it was very urgent, the man became much more helpful. 'You'll have to go to the top of the cliffs,' he said as he put his bucket down on the mud. 'There's some steps up a little way south-east from here.' The Five all thanked him, quickly looking for their compasses.

Use your COMPASS CARD to find south-east by placing exactly over the shape below – and with pointer touching north. Then go to the number that appears in the window. If you don't have one, you'll have to guess which of the numbers to go to.

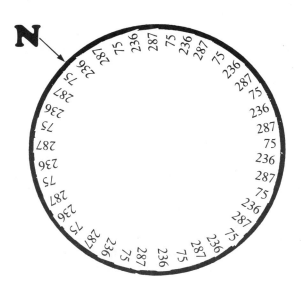

228

When the children took out their torches, however, they found that they were all virtually flat! 'I'm afraid we've used them so much today,' Julian apologised to the sergeant, 'that there's hardly a flicker left!' Fortunately, the moon soon reappeared from behind a large cloud and the boat's pilot could just about find his way by that. *Go to 265.*

229

Just as they were about to pick their blades of grass, however, they heard a voice from behind. It was Wilfrid running after them! 'I forgot to tell you the way down to the beach,' he said, out of breath, 'you might never find it otherwise.' He told them that they should head for the tall flagpost in the distance, then turn due west. They asked him once more if he would like to come but he said he daren't. So they said goodbye to him again, hurrying towards the flagpost. When they reached it, they started looking for their compasses in their rucksacks so they could find where west was.

Do you have a COMPASS in your RUCKSACK? If so, use it to find out which direction to go by placing exactly over the shape

below – and with pointer touching north. Then go to the number that appears in the window. (Remember to put the CARD back in your RUCKSACK afterwards.) If you don't have a COMPASS CARD, you'll have to guess which of the numbers to go to.

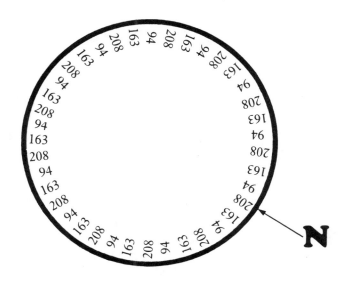

230

Dick steered the boat towards the left end of the island, giving little tugs on the rudder. 'How much further is it?' Julian asked when he had been rowing for a good half hour, 'I'm getting puffed out.' Dick told him it was still a fair way to go, though, and so they agreed to swap places to give Julian a rest. Dick hadn't been rowing for long when they entered a sudden mist. 'Oh no,' cried Anne, 'we'll never find the island now!' The only one who didn't seem worried was George. 'That's because I secretly checked the island against my compass before it disappeared,' she boasted. She insisted that they all said how clever she was before she told them that it was in a north-westerly direction.

Use your COMPASS CARD to find this direction by placing

exactly over the shape below – and with pointer touching north.
Then go to the number that appears in the window. If you don't
have a COMPASS in your RUCKSACK, you'll have to guess
which of the numbers to go to.

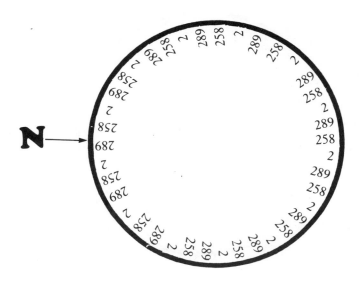

231

They were still excitedly searching for their codebooks when Anne
gave a sudden scream! 'Look out,' she cried to Julian, 'there's a
sharp point sticking out of the water just in front!' Julian was only
just able to avoid it, desperately back-pedalling with the oars. 'How
stupid I am,' he said when they were a safe distance away, 'I forgot
that buoys often mark something dangerous in the water!' It was
only when the boat was safely ashore on the beach that Anne made a
confession to them all. Seeing that sharp point had given her such a
fright that she accidentally threw her compass over the side!

If you have it, remove the COMPASS CARD from your
RUCKSACK. Now go to 54.

In the end it wasn't one of The Five's suggestions they followed at all – but Wilfrid's! He noticed some stone steps leading up to the battlements and he said they would get a bird's-eye view of the castle from up there. When they had reached the top of the crumbling steps, Anne pointed out an iron grid across the ground in the far corner of the courtyard. 'I wonder what that's for?' she said. 'It looks like the cover for some sort of hole.' Just before they went down to investigate, George noticed an old flagpost standing on the cliff edge in the distance. She suggested they should look it up on their maps so they would know which part of the island this was.

Use your MAP CARD to find which square the flagpost is in – then follow the instruction. If you don't have a map, you'll have to guess which instruction to follow.

If you think D1	go to 302
If you think C1	go to 268
If you think E1	go to 139

233

Quickly flicking through the codebook's pages before she forgot what was on the brick, George told the others what the message worked out as. 'It says that the well is a lot more than it seems,' she told them, scratching her head. The others scratched their heads as well, wondering what it meant exactly. 'Well, we can't stand here puzzling about it all day,' said Julian, preparing to set off again. 'We've got that castle to find!' *Go to 56.*

As they tried to wriggle off their rucksacks, however, Anne slipped over the edge! The others were just able to grab hold of her arms in time and pull her back. They agreed that looking for their codebooks was too dangerous and so they would just have to forget decoding the message. Before they continued down the cliff steps, Anne opened her lunchbox to check her bottle of ginger beer hadn't broken. Miraculously, it hadn't – but her cake had crumbled into so many tiny pieces that she decided just to throw them away for the gulls.

Take one PICNIC CARD from your LUNCHBOX. Now go to 270.

The others said there wasn't time to look for their codebooks, however – it was much more important that they reached their boat quickly. So Dick left the wallet on the ground, hurrying to catch the others up. It was only much later that he realised his compass must have fallen out when he had bent down for the wallet.

If you have it, remove the COMPASS CARD from your RUCKSACK. Now go to 12.

Following their compasses, they soon found the steps the man had described. They were just about to climb up when the man came running after them. 'Perhaps you could hand this map in to the police station when you're there,' he said. 'I found it on the beach but I haven't the time to give it in myself. I've got far too many cockles to collect!' Saying they would be happy to oblige, The Five took the map with them.

If you don't already have it, put the MAP CARD into your RUCKSACK. Now go to 145.

Switching his torch on, Julian pointed it in exactly the same direction as the boat's spotlight so they could see where they were going again. In fact, the sergeant said it was probably better than the spotlight since it wouldn't make them so obvious. 'If the gang see us first,' he told them with a little anxiety in his voice, 'they might have a chance to get away!' *Go to 265.*

Unfortunately, the monument wasn't shown on their maps and so they still didn't know whether they were going the right way or not. 'We'll just have to hope that we are,' said Julian as they continued along the path again. It wasn't long, though, before the path began to turn downwards and they saw some bright yellow sand below. With a great cheer, they all quickened their step. *Go to 66.*

'Well done, Anne,' said the others as she pointed out a small sandy cove just before the next bend, 'that looks perfect!' They were soon pulling the boat up on to the shore and giving their legs a good stretch. 'That's better,' said Dick, 'I was beginning to worry that I would never be able to walk properly again!' Timmy was giving his legs a good stretch too, running up and down the beach, but then he suddenly stopped. 'What is it, Timmy?' George asked, noticing him sniff at a patch of damp sand. They all ran up to him to have a look and saw that someone had scratched a message there! *SHOULD YOU NEED TO FLASH A SIGNAL*, it read, *WALK 15 PACES SOUTH-EAST*. Mystified, the children quickly hurried back to the boat to fetch their compasses!

Do you have a COMPASS? If so, use it to find out which direction south-east is by placing exactly over the shape below – and with pointer touching north. Then go to the number that

***appears in the window. If you don't have a COMPASS CARD,
you'll have to guess which of the numbers to go to.***

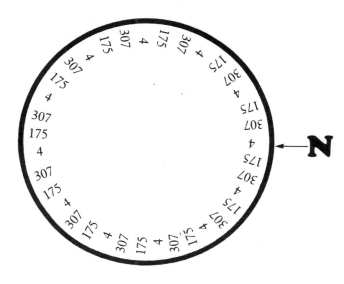

240

The wood became darker and darker, noisier and noisier, as Anne
led the way along the path. It was a bit frightening going first but she
decided it was a lot better than going last. At least she didn't have to
worry about what was behind her this way! After about half an hour
or so, they suddenly noticed a clearing in front. They could just see
some slabs of stone there and they hurried up to them, thinking this
might be the remains of the castle. When they got there, however,
they discovered that it was an old graveyard. They started to look it
up on their maps so that they would know where they were.

***Use your MAP CARD to find which square the old graveyard is
in – then follow the instruction. If you don't have one, you'll have
to guess which instruction to follow.***

If you think C1	go to 6
If you think C2	go to 124
If you think C3	go to 55

Julian, being the eldest, thought he had better volunteer and so he tested the rope to make sure it would take his weight. The others then carefully lowered him down, waiting for him to shout 'stop'. Not only did he come back with Anne's rucksack but also a scrap of paper! 'Look, there's a message on it!' he said, handing it to the others. *FOR THE CASTLE*, Dick, George and Anne eagerly read together, *GO NORTH-EAST FROM HERE*. As soon as they had helped Julian brush himself down, they all started looking for their compasses!

Use your COMPASS CARD to find this direction yourself by placing exactly over the shape below – and with pointer touching north. Then go to the number that appears in the window. If you don't have a COMPASS, you'll have to guess which of the numbers to go to.

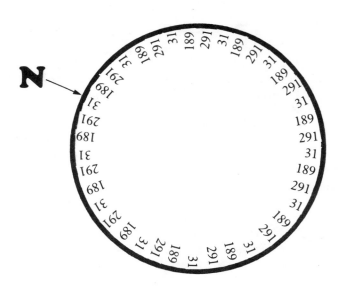

'Look, there's something in the third hole from the right!' Dick shouted as their torches flashed all round the roof. Luckily, it was one of the lower holes and Dick was just able to reach it by standing on Julian's shoulders. They all eagerly waited for Dick to show them what he had found but it was just an old map of the island. Then Anne thought it might have a clue to where the treasure was and so they decided to take it with them. Just as they were folding it up to put it in one of their rucksacks, Timmy sniffed out a secret trap door in the floor. 'It must lead down to the dungeons!' Julian exclaimed as they discovered a dark stairway underneath.

If you don't already have it, put the MAP CARD into your RUCKSACK. Now go to 190.

Their maps flapped so wildly in the wind, however, that it was impossible to read them. As George was putting hers away again, she accidentally pulled out her compass. It started to roll towards the edge! 'Quick, try and stop it!' she screamed to the others, but it was too late – it had gone over! Seconds later, they could just hear it smash into pieces against a rock at the bottom!

If you have it, remove the COMPASS CARD from your RUCKSACK. Now go to 270.

They were still waiting for someone brave enough to go first when they heard a piercing cry from the cave. They all dashed behind some rocks, wondering what it was. 'Perhaps it's haunted,' said Wilfrid, beginning to wish that he hadn't decided to come along after all! They then saw two gulls fly out from the cave, however, and realised that the cry had just been from them. 'What cowards we all are!' laughed Dick as they at last went inside. They could feel a slight draught of air from the very back of the cave and they went towards it, discovering a narrow opening in the rock. Squeezing through, they found themselves at the beginning of a long, dark tunnel. 'We had better use our torches,' said Julian.

Use your TORCH CARD to light up the way by placing exactly over the shape below – then follow the instruction. If you don't have one, go to 224 instead.

```
L G  GT M O  H R   E E O R S   T H   Z   O
  E   O   T   E   W   N E   J    ! T D   O   E E
    S  C F I  E V    T   S    X O     E   S E   N
    Z  N     O  $  S   E     I  R  N       E K X  M
```

'Look, we've come back to the castle dungeons again!' Julian exclaimed on recognising the large chamber where they had been before. There were the same rusty manacles and the old-fashioned torches built into the wall. The only thing that was missing were the crates of treasure! Then Julian suddenly realised what was going on. He said that the men had been illegally collecting all the island's treasures and storing them down here. The time had now come to take them off the island and so they had carried them along the secret tunnel to wait for a boat at the cave. 'We must hurry back to the mainland,' he quickly finished, 'and inform the police so they'll be able to stop the operation!' Just as they were about to climb up the dungeon steps to the outside, however, one of the men started coming down them with a gun! *Go to 143.*

246

They were in the middle of taking their maps out when Dick said there was no need. He remembered the statue from when they were coming and it was about half way on the journey. They hadn't gone much further when disaster struck! George suddenly pulled on the rudder a bit too hard and the jolt caused Anne to knock her lunchbox over the side. Anne sadly watched it sink out of sight!

Take one PICNIC CARD from your LUNCHBOX. Now go to 13.

247

George had noticed a horse-rider out for an evening gallop further along the beach and her suggestion was to go and ask him. 'You're looking for the police station, you say?' the man asked as he brought his horse to a halt. 'Well, first of all you need to go to the top of the cliffs. I believe there are a series of steps five or six minutes' walk south-east from here.' Before he had told them where south-east was, however, the man had galloped off again. They would just have to look it up on their compasses!

Use your COMPASS CARD to find south-east by placing exactly over the shape below – and with pointer touching north. Then go to the number that appears in the window. If you don't have one, you'll have to guess which of the numbers to go to.

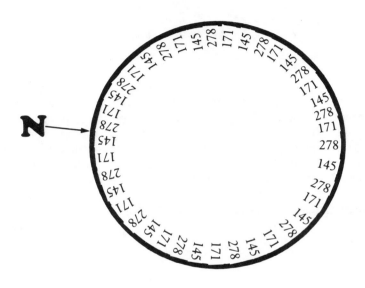

248

It wasn't much longer before they were approaching the cave and the sergeant ordered the pilot to switch off the engine and dim the lights. 'We'll wait here and quietly watch what happens,' he said. To help pass the time while they were waiting, Dick offered round the remainder of his cake. 'If all goes well, it will be a long time before those gang members are eating cake again!' the sergeant exclaimed with a chuckle.

Take one PICNIC CARD from your LUNCHBOX. Now go to 93.

249

All shining their torches in the same direction, they lit up a small hole through the mist. 'Our torches will also make it a lot easier for other boats to see us,' said Julian. And just to be extra sure that other boats realised they were there, Dick started to make a noise like a fog-horn! The others were in the middle of laughing at this strange sound when Anne suddenly noticed a small, shiny object at the bottom of the boat. 'Look, it's a compass!' she exclaimed. 'It must have been dropped by one of the previous hirers.'

If you don't already have it, put the COMPASS CARD into your RUCKSACK. Now go to 2.

250

They were just laughing about how lucky they were to have encountered this strong wind – it had been a lot easier than rowing – when Anne suddenly noticed their rucksacks. The spray had made them wet through! They quickly lifted them out of the boat to check their contents. Luckily, the wetness was mainly on the outside of the rucksacks and hadn't got through to the inside. The only thing that was ruined was George's codebook. She had kept it in a special pocket at the front and it was now in soggy little pieces!

If you have it, remove the CODEBOOK CARD from your RUCKSACK. Now go to 54.

They still hadn't quite agreed who was to lead the way through the wood when a raven hopped up to them, pecking at Dick's shoe. They were just saying how tame it was when George had a brilliant idea! She remembered that ravens often liked to live near old buildings and if they followed it, it might lead them to the castle. So she ordered Timmy to give a loud bark to make it fly off. The trouble was, the raven flew through the trees so quickly that they had difficulty keeping up with it. 'I know,' said George with another idea, 'let's check which way it's flying on our compasses. Then we'll know the right direction even after it's disappeared.'

Use your COMPASS CARD to work out the raven's direction by placing exactly over the shape below – and with pointer touching north. Then go to the number that appears in the window. If you don't have a COMPASS CARD, you'll have to guess which of the numbers to go to.

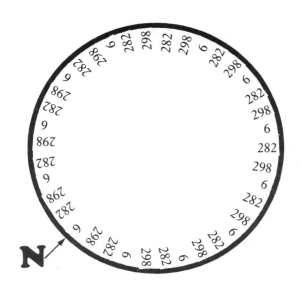

252

By the time George had reached the top of the well again, however, she had forgotten most of the message. Being in code, it was difficult to remember! 'Perhaps I should go down again with a codebook this time,' she suggested but Julian said that it would mean holding on to the rope with one hand and it wasn't worth the risk. So they decided to continue looking for the castle but, before they did, George had a quick drink of her ginger beer. All that hanging on to the rope had made her thirsty!

Take one PICNIC CARD from your LUNCHBOX. Now go to 56.

253

They all crept behind George to the top of the steps and then dashed back into the wood. When they tried to find their way to the coast, however, they became just as lost as before. Suddenly, Wilfrid spotted a curious-looking stone tower through the trees ahead. As they approached, they saw that there was a stairway inside leading up to the top. 'I think it's what's known as a folly,' said Julian. 'People of old often used to build these strange monuments to amuse themselves.' He then suggested that he should climb up to see if he could spot the cliffs. Finally reaching the top, he found that he *could* just see them and he looked for his compass so he would know their direction.

Use your COMPASS CARD to check the cliffs' direction by placing exactly over the shape below – and with pointer touching north. Then go to the number that appears in the window. If you don't have one, you'll have to guess which of the numbers to go to.

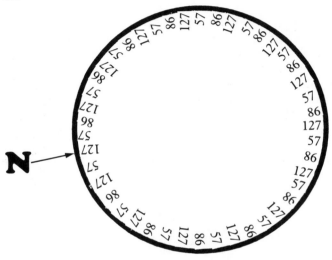

254

'We can see where we're going now!' Julian remarked as his torch lit up right along the tunnel. They had only turned the next bend when he spotted a large sheet of paper on the tunnel's rocky floor. 'Look, it's a map of the island!' he exclaimed on picking it up. 'It must have been dropped by one of those men.' Taking a closer look at the map, they noticed that there were a number of crosses drawn on it. In case it might help the police work out what the men were up to, they decided to take it with them.

If you don't already have it, put the MAP CARD into your RUCKSACK. Now go to 142.

255

Switching it on, Julian quickly shone his torch on each of the signpost's arms. The first read *TO THE CHURCH*, the second *TO THE COASTGUARDS* and the third . . . *TO THE POLICE STATION*! 'It must be that building over there!' exclaimed Dick, pointing to where a tiny blue light was shining in the distance. As they hurried towards it, Timmy suddenly stopped to sniff at something in the short grass. It was a secret codebook! 'Perhaps that means one of the gang lives on the mainland!' exclaimed Julian, as they took it with them to show to the police.

*If you don't already have it, put the **CODEBOOK CARD** into your **RUCKSACK**. Now go to 119.*

256

Fortunately, the anchor-monument *was* shown on their maps and they could now tell where they were. When they then looked to see if a police station was also shown, however, they found there wasn't one. 'Blow,' exclaimed Dick, 'it must be off the edge! We'll just have to try and find it some other way!' *Go to 25.*

257

It was decided Julian should point the way, since he was the eldest. 'When you reach the island,' he told the pilot, 'just keep following the coast round to the right.' The motor-boat went at top speed and it wasn't long before it was approaching the part with the cave. 'We'd better switch off all the boat's lights so as not to alert them,' said the sergeant as they now went much more slowly. He asked if anyone had a torch they could use instead.

*Use your **TORCH CARD** to provide some light by placing exactly over the shape below – then follow the instruction. If you don't have one, go to 228 instead.*

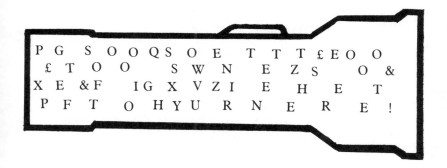

```
P  G   S  O  O Q S   O  E    T  T  T £ E O   O
   £ T  O   O      S  W  N     E  Z S        O  &
X  E  & F    I G  X  V Z I    E    H   E     T
   P  F  T    O  H Y U   R   N    E    R      E   !
```

258
They suddenly realised there was a problem, however. Their compasses were still in their rucksacks and they were wedged into the far end of the boat. If they tried to reach them, they might turn the boat over. 'We'll just have to stop here until the mist clears,' said Dick, lifting out his oars. 'Let's hope we don't drift too much.' **Go to 2.**

259
Timmy led them, with his tongue eagerly hanging out, to a crumbling stone keep at the far side of the courtyard. Inside there was a large iron drum with a handle on it. Wrapped round the drum was a stout chain which led to a hole high up in the wall. 'This must be the mechanism for opening the drawbridge,' said Dick,

remembering that he had seen a large gateway just outside the keep. When they turned the drum a little, they noticed a message chalked on to it! It was in code, though, and so they quickly started digging through their rucksacks for a codebook.

*Use your **CODEBOOK CARD** to find out what the message said by decoding the instruction below. If you don't have one, go to 292 instead.*

260

They all stayed close behind as Anne led them into the heart of the cave. She was really quite nervous going first but she thought it only right that she took the risks sometimes. She soon felt a slight draught of air on her face and she followed it to a narrow opening at the very back of the cave. They all squeezed through, finding themselves at the beginning of a long, dark tunnel. 'We'd better use our torches to help us see,' said Julian, beginning to feel through his rucksack.

*Use your **TORCH CARD** to light up the way by placing exactly*

*over the shape below – then follow the instruction. If you don't
have one, go to 224 instead.*

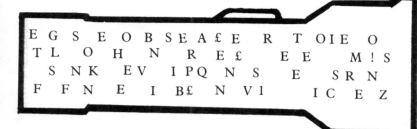

```
E G S  E  O B S E A £ E   R  T  OIE  O
T L  O  H  N  R E £     E E     M ! S
  S N K  EV  I P Q  N  S    E   S R N
F  F F N  E  I  B £  N  V I        IC  E  Z
```

261
The coded message said that the boat was to arrive just after
midnight. 'It must have been written by one of those men who were
piling up the boxes,' said Julian – although still not fully understand-
ing what it was all about. Perhaps when they had explored the cave
they would have a much better idea! **Go to 270.**

262
To begin with, they tried to make their way without their torches to
save their batteries for later. Instead, they just felt along the passage
wall. But then they heard a slight scurrying noise ahead and Anne

became worried about rats. 'Okay Anne, we'll use one of our torches,' Julian said. It wasn't just for Anne's sake, though. Although he would never admit it, Julian was a little edgy about rats himself!

Use your TORCH CARD to see what the noise was by placing exactly over the shape below – then follow the instruction. If you don't have one, go to 10 instead.

```
S G D  S O T E   I  Z X E  T  R Y O
@  E T R  W Z T E      O  F N    X  E
Z O   T   N  P I Z  N  E    E   R Q   J
  E!!  T LI  H  G  R L H  E    T   E M
```

263

As soon as one of them had found a torch, they shone it back down the passage. The man was still nowhere in sight and so they decided to risk climbing the rope. They suddenly realised there was the problem of Timmy but then Julian had the brilliant idea of squeezing him into his rucksack! It was only when they had reached the top of the shaft that they recognised where they were. It was the well where they had stopped before! After pulling up the rope so the man couldn't follow them, they hurriedly set off back towards where they had hidden their boat. On the way, Wilfrid noticed a map of the island on the ground. Just in case it showed more than their own maps, they decided to take it with them.

If you don't already have it, put the MAP CARD into your RUCKSACK. Now go to 12.

Julian had noticed a night-time fisherman about to take his boat out and his idea was to go and ask him. 'Excuse me,' he said, as they all hurried up to him, 'but can you tell us the way to the police station? It's urgent!' The fisherman scratched his head for a moment before answering. 'Well, let me see . . .' he said, 'yes, there's one on the cliff-tops. Now you'll be wanting to know how to get up the cliffs, I suppose? There's a little path three minutes' walk south-east from here.' The Five immediately searched for their compasses!

Use your COMPASS CARD to find south-east by placing exactly over the shape below – and with pointer touching north. Then go to the number that appears in the window. If you don't have one, you'll have to guess which of the numbers to go to.

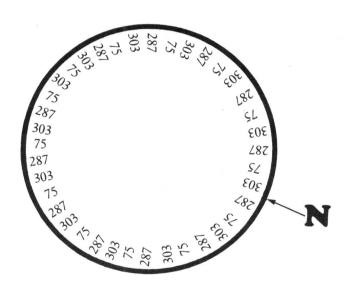

The police boat continued quietly chugging through the water as they looked out for the cave. Finally, they spotted it – and the pilot switched off the engine altogether. 'Look, there are the men!' Julian whispered excitedly, pointing to three or four small shadowy figures

standing just outside the cave. 'The boat to collect them is obviously
due any minute!' he added. While they were waiting, the sergeant
asked the children to show him where the cave was on their maps for
when he wrote his report. So they hurriedly started searching
through their rucksacks!

*Use your MAP CARD to find which square the cave is in – then
follow the instruction. If you don't have one, you'll have to guess
which instruction to follow.*

If you think D1	go to 134
If you think D3	go to 107
If you think D2	go to 51

266

Julian hadn't been steering for long when a sudden mist appeared.
Within seconds, it had completely surrounded them! They wondered what they were going to do, worried that they might crash into
another boat and sink. Then George had an idea. They could all put
their torches on to make it easier to see. 'It's a good job we
remembered to bring them along,' said Dick as they started
searching for them in their rucksacks.

*Do you have a TORCH in your RUCKSACK? If so, use it to
light up the way by placing exactly over the shape below – then
follow the instruction. (Remember to put the CARD back in your
RUCKSACK afterwards.) If you don't have a TORCH CARD,
go to 280 instead.*

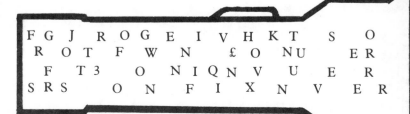

```
F G J   R O G   E   I   V   H   K T     S     O
  R   O T   F   W   N     £   O   N U       E R
    F   T 3     O   N I Q N   V     U     E     R
S R S       O   N   F   I   X   N     V     E   R
```

Normally, the boys couldn't have resisted going for a quick swim but this lake looked such a peculiar colour that they didn't fancy it. Instead of being blue, it was a horrible dark green! So they continued on their way, soon in the depths of the wood again. It wasn't until they had left the lake far behind that Julian realised his codebook was missing. 'Drat!' he exclaimed. 'It must have fallen out of my rucksack when we were sitting on that log.'

If you have it, remove the CODEBOOK CARD from your RUCKSACK. Now go to 30.

The others said it was much too windy to open their maps up there, however, and they could study them later. So they immediately returned to the bottom of the steps and hurried over to where they had seen the grid in the ground. 'Look, there's a stairway underneath!' Julian exclaimed. 'It must lead down to the castle dungeons.' The grid lifted up and so they decided to follow the steps. Before they started however, they all had some of their ginger beer for courage!

Take one PICNIC CARD from your LUNCHBOX. Now go to 190.

Before they had decided who was to go first down the steps, however, one of the men reappeared from the cave. He seemed to be writing something on one of the crates. They waited until he had gone back again before starting the steep climb down. When they had finally reached the narrow stretch of beach at the bottom, they hurried over to the crates to see what the writing said. 'Oh blow,' exclaimed Anne, 'it's in code! We'll have to take out our code-books.'

Use your CODEBOOK CARD to find out what the message said by decoding the instruction below. If you don't have one, go to 21 instead.

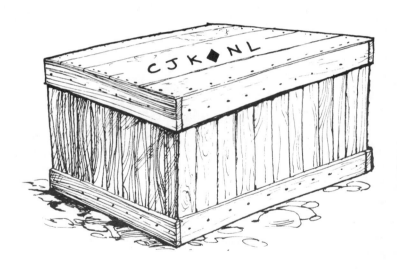

A few more to go and they at last reached the bottom of the steps. They walked along the thin stretch of sand to the entrance to the cave. They were just about to venture inside when Timmy noticed that someone had written a message in the sand with his foot. *BOAT WILL BE COMING FROM SIR HENRY'S POINT*, it read. They wondered where Sir Henry's Point was, but then Wilfrid remembered that there was a statue to Sir Henry on the island. 'So that's probably where his "Point" is!' he remarked. The problem was – *where was the statue*? They hurriedly looked for their maps to find out!

Use your MAP CARD to find which square the statue is in – then follow the instruction. If you don't have one, you'll have to guess which number to go to.

If you think A4	go to 34
If you think B4	go to 89
If you think A3	go to 313

271

'I can't see anyone down there,' said Julian as he shone his torch into the well. '*I can't see anyone down there*,' a voice suddenly came back at him. Then they all realised what it was they had heard. It was just an echo of themselves! 'What idiots we all are!' Dick laughed as they set off through the wood. *Go to 60.*

Timmy insisted on doing the steering, working the rope with his teeth! 'A little bit to the left,' said Julian as he started pulling on the oars, 'now a little bit to the right.' Timmy had soon steered them clear of the shallows and they now headed back towards the mainland. It was becoming so dark, however, that they were worried that they might be hit by another boat. Dick then suggested switching on one of their torches to warn others that they were there.

Use your TORCH CARD to help the boat be seen by placing exactly over the shape below – then follow the instruction. If you don't have one, go to 226 instead.

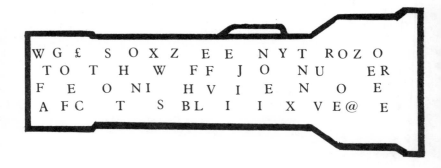

The trick worked! After a short delay, another flash appeared from the island! 'So there *is* someone still living there!' Dick exclaimed with a mixture of fear and excitement. The only one who didn't join in the excitement was Timmy. He was busy sniffing round the bottom of the boat. 'What have you found, Timmy?' George asked when he started to tug at a piece of paper wedged under one of the seats. Helping him to pull the paper free, she noticed that it was a map of the island! Although they already had maps with them, this one looked more detailed and so they decided to take it as well.

If you don't already have it, put the MAP CARD into your RUCKSACK. Now go to 41.

274

As soon as Dick was high enough, George handed him the torch that Timmy had fetched. He was then lowered down again. 'I feel like a yo-yo,' he laughed from inside the well as he switched the torch on. The hole became a lot brighter with the torch and it wasn't long before he spotted the rucksack, floating on the water at the bottom. 'You were lucky the water didn't have time to soak in,' he told Anne as he handed it back to her a few minutes later. Before they had any further mishaps at the well, they continued on their way! *Go to 56.*

275

They had been walking along the cliff-top for quite some time now but the cave was still nowhere to be seen. 'Let's stop for a short rest,' said Dick, 'I feel as if my legs are about to give way!' Once they were sitting down, they couldn't resist having some of their picnic as well. The lush green grass and the beautiful view made it one of the best picnic spots they had ever seen!

Take one PICNIC CARD from your LUNCHBOX. Now go to 9.

The tunnel a lot brighter now, they started to follow it. 'Do you always have adventures like this?' Wilfrid asked on the way. 'Yes, a lot of the time,' the others answered with a chuckle. 'We can't seem to help it!' ***Go to 142.***

They were just opening their codebooks when George noticed that Anne's hair was slightly blowing. That must mean there was a draught from somewhere – probably from the tunnel! When they all searched behind Anne, they found that George was right. There was a narrow opening in the cave wall! They started to walk down the tunnel but it was much longer than they expected and they stopped after half an hour for a quick bite to eat. Two or three hundred metres further, the tunnel finally came to an end at a large wooden door. They slowly opened it, wondering what was on the other side . . .

Take one PICNIC CARD from your LUNCHBOX. Now go to 245. (Remember: when there are no picnic cards left in your lunchbox, the game is over and you must start again.)

Before they had taken their compasses out, however, they heard the horse-rider calling back at them from over his shoulder. 'Yes, I was right,' he yelled as he galloped along, '– there are the steps, over there!' His arm pointed to the place for a few seconds before returning to the reins. Shouting a 'thank you' after him, The Five then hurried towards the spot. Climbing the steps proved such hard work, however, that George insisted on a rest half way up to have some of her ginger beer.

Take one PICNIC CARD from your LUNCHBOX. Now go to 145.

279
The message said that the children had escaped and everyone was to be on the look-out for them so they couldn't leave the island. 'It must be talking about us,' exclaimed Dick with anxiety, '– and was written by one of those men to warn the others!' It must also have been written fairly recently which meant that the person might not be far away! 'Quick, back to the boat in case he suddenly reappears!' ordered Julian and they hurriedly rowed out to sea. It was only when the island was a good distance behind them that they felt sure they were safe. ***Go to 76.***

280
The mist was so thick, however, that the torches weren't much use. They decided to put them away again, trying to think of a way to warn other boats that they were there. 'If only we had a fog-horn,' said Julian, 'then we wouldn't have to worry.' There was an anxious silence for a short while, then George suddenly gave a cry of inspiration. 'We *do* have a fog-horn,' she said excitedly, '– right in

this boat!' The others all thought she had gone a bit crazy but then she told them what she meant. 'The fog-horn's called Timmy!' she explained laughingly. 'All he has to do is keep barking at the top of his voice!' ***Go to 2.***

281

They had only rowed a few metres further when the boat suddenly stopped! 'What's happened?' asked Dick, pulling really hard on his oar. 'I can't get the boat to move!' When he brought the oar up again, however, he noticed that the tip was covered with wet sand. They must have hit a sand-bank! Julian and Dick both dug their oars in as deeply as they could, trying to push the boat away. Suddenly, they were free again – but it happened with such a jerk that Dick's rucksack fell over the edge! He was just able to grab hold of it before it sank. When he tested his torch, however, he found that some water had leaked in and it no longer worked.

If you have it, remove the TORCH CARD from your RUCK-SACK. Now go to 41.

282

'We can stop to catch our breath now,' said George when their compasses showed that the raven was flying in a north-easterly direction. The raven soon vanished into the dense trees but it didn't matter because they could just follow their compasses from now on. On the way, Anne suddenly noticed an old book on the ground, half covered by some leaves. 'Look, it's a codebook!' she told the others. After brushing the dirt off, they decided to take it with them in case it was a different type to theirs.

If you don't already have it, put the CODEBOOK CARD into your RUCKSACK. Now go to 188.

283

While the others were looking for their codebooks, Julian gave the bucket a bit of a rub with his hand to make the message clearer. Suddenly though, the bottom crumbled away. It was so rusty that it tore just like paper! 'It's a good job it didn't fall to pieces while Timmy was in it,' George remarked as they disappointedly put their codebooks away again. They had soon left the well, Dick not realising that he had forgotten to repack his map!

If you have it, remove the MAP CARD from your RUCKSACK. Now go to 113.

As soon as they switched their torches on, they noticed something sparkle back at them from some boxes in the corner. 'Hey, look – gold plates,' shouted Wilfrid as they hurried over to them, 'masses and masses of them!' They had just started to examine one of the plates when they heard two men's voices coming down the steps. 'Quick, crouch behind one of the boxes!' Julian whispered to the others. 'They don't sound the type to give us a warm welcome!' *Go to 155.*

Having followed Julian to the top of the steps, they all crept across the castle courtyard and back into the wood again. They could hear the distant cry of gulls to their right and they turned in that direction, guessing that's where the cliffs would be. When they reached the cliff-top, they decided to keep following it round until they spotted the cave. On their way, Anne noticed a small outcrop of rock just out to sea. She suggested they look it up on their maps so they would know how much further to walk.

Use your MAP CARD to find which square the outcrop of rock is in – then follow the instruction. If you don't have one, you'll have to guess which instruction to follow.

If you think E1	go to 168
If you think E2	go to 202
If you think D2	go to 46

'North-east is in the direction of that small outcrop of rock over there,' said Dick, pointing out to sea. 'I still can't think what this boat could be up to, though,' he added as he put his compass away again. They had only climbed down a few steps more when Wilfrid noticed that part of the rock he had put his hand on was loose. 'It seems to be some sort of hiding place,' he said as he pulled a neat square of it out. He was right! Behind the square fragment of rock was a hole. And when he put his arm in, he found a codebook!

If you don't already have it, put the CODEBOOK CARD into your RUCKSACK. Now go to 270.

They were still looking for their compasses when Wilfrid gave his head a sudden smack! 'How silly I am,' he exclaimed, 'I've suddenly realised I know this part myself! I can find you the path up the cliff without your compasses!' He led them along the beach a little, stopping at where the cliffs were at their lowest. 'There it is,' he said, pointing to a series of narrow wooden steps set into the rock. It was such a steep climb up the steps, however, that George insisted on a rest half way up so she could have some of her ginger beer.

Take one PICNIC CARD from your LUNCHBOX. Now go to 145.

Before anyone had time to offer, however, George distracted their attention. 'Look,' she exclaimed, pointing a little further up the beach, 'someone's scratched a message into the sand!' They all ran up to it to find out what it said but as they got nearer they realised that it was in some sort of code. 'I'll go back to the boat to fetch the codebook from my rucksack!' volunteered Dick.

Use your CODEBOOK CARD to find out what the message said by decoding the instruction below. If you don't have one, go to 61 instead.

C J D ◆ N Z F

Having found north-west on his compass, Julian pulled on the rudder until the boat pointed the same way. He then told Dick to start gently rowing again. After a few minutes or so, Dick's oar suddenly hit something hard in the water. 'Look, it's a plastic box,' he said, carefully scooping it up. When they took off the lid, they saw that there was an old codebook inside. Although Wilfrid had lent them each a codebook, they decided to take this one as well in case it was a different type.

If you don't already have it, put the CODEBOOK CARD into your RUCKSACK. Now go to 2.

They were just about to switch their torches on when the wood suddenly became a little lighter again. The odd patch of sky started to appear between the leaves. They therefore decided to save their torches for later, in case they were in more need of them then. Ahead, a shaft of sunlight lit up a circle of mossy ground and it seemed the perfect spot for a picnic. 'The wood doesn't seem quite so scary now, does it?' said Dick as, bathed in the sun's golden rays, he happily munched on a sandwich.

Take one PICNIC CARD from your LUNCHBOX. Now go to 188.

They hadn't walked far when a tame rabbit hopped up to them. 'It shows how unused to humans the animals in this wood are,' exclaimed George. 'It doesn't even know to be wary of us!' Timmy just couldn't understand it. Normally, rabbits ran *away* from him – not *towards* him. In fact, he was so puzzled by it that he lost all of his bark for a moment! Anne was so delighted by the friendly creature that she gave it the lettuce and cucumber from one of her salad sandwiches.

Take one PICNIC CARD from your LUNCHBOX. Now go to 56.

They were just about to begin decoding the chalked message when they saw that it had gone! Then Anne noticed that Timmy's coat had a white dust on it. 'Oh no,' she said, 'Timmy must have accidentally brushed against the drum and wiped the message off. Silly dog!' They thought he was sulking because he suddenly went over to the corner but then they realised he had sniffed out a secret stairway in the floor. 'It must lead to the dungeons!' said Julian with excitement as they started to climb down. On the way, Anne gave Timmy a piece of her cake to show that he wasn't such a silly dog after all!

Take one PICNIC CARD from your LUNCHBOX. Now go to 190.

293

They were less than half way through decoding the message, when it suddenly caught fire! In their excitement, they had held it just a bit too near the torch's flames! 'We're just going to have to try and find the cave ourselves,' said George disappointedly. They crept back into the woods and eventually emerged at the cliff-tops. 'The best idea is just to keep following the cliffs round,' said Julian. After a whole hour of walking, though, they wondered how much further they had to go before spotting the cave. The cliffs just seemed to lead on and on! 'I vote we stop for some of our picnic before going any further,' said Dick wearily. The rest happily agreed, feeling much more refreshed after a sandwich or two!

Take one PICNIC CARD from your LUNCHBOX. Now go to 9.

By the time they had found their codebooks, however, the letters had become too far away to see. Their boat must have been carried a bit by a current. Dick wanted to row back again but Julian said there wasn't time. 'It's much more important that we get to the police first,' he said. The salty air was soon making everyone so thirsty that George offered round her ginger beer.

Take one PICNIC CARD from your LUNCHBOX. Now go to 13.

295

Just as that moment, though, it started to pour with rain! 'It looks like it's just a quick burst,' said George staring up into the dark sky, 'so I suggest we leave taking out our maps until afterwards or they'll be ruined.' While they were waiting for the rain to stop, they all shared some of Julian's sandwiches.

Take one PICNIC CARD from your LUNCHBOX. Now go to 25.

296

'They should easily be able to see us now!' said Julian as his torch shone across the water. He gave it to Anne to hold so that he could return to the rowing. 'I hope the batteries don't suddenly run down,' she remarked, knowing how much they had used them already on this adventure. *Go to 76.*

Before anyone spotted a bay, a sudden wind blew up, blinding them with spray. 'I can't see a thing,' cried Julian anxiously, 'I hope I'm not heading straight for the cliffs!' There was nothing he could do about it, though, because the boat now seemed to have a will of its own, charging through the water. 'Oh no, we've had it!' George cried as it suddenly flung them all out. But instead of landing in the cold sea as they expected, they fell on soft dry sand. They had found a bay after all! As soon as they had dragged the boat clear of the water, Julian suggested they look up this sandy beach on their maps so they would know where they were.

Use your MAP CARD to find which square the sandy bay is in – then follow the instruction. If you don't have a MAP CARD in your RUCKSACK, you'll have to guess which instruction to follow.

If you think A1	go to 54
If you think A2	go to 250
If you think A3	go to 187

They weren't quick enough, though, because the raven had vanished into the dense trees before they could take their compasses out. 'We'll just have to guess the way,' said Julian, looking round. 'Let's hope we can find that path again!' Before they went a step further, however, they decided to have a quick drink of their ginger beer. Running after that raven had made them so hot that they needed something to cool them down!

Take one PICNIC CARD from your LUNCHBOX. Now go to 188.

Just as they were about to read their compasses, however, Anne noticed a thin line of light from the far end of the cavern. It looked like the slit that you see at the edge of a door. Tip-toeing towards it, they found that it *was* a door – disguised to look like some of the rock. There was even a key-hole in it! 'So this is where they left by!' Julian whispered. They waited for the men's voices to move away before trying the door. Luckily, it hadn't been locked and so they slowly pushed it open, wondering what was on the other side . . .
Go to 245.

It was so dangerous trying to look through their rucksacks on this narrow cliff-edge, however, that they decided not to take their compasses out after all. It was hardly worth falling to the bottom for! They had walked a little further down the steps when they suddenly became aware of someone following them. Turning round, they saw that it was a flock of seagulls quietly pecking in their footsteps. To begin with, they wondered what they were eating but then George suddenly realised. 'Oh, no,' she cried, 'my lunchbox wasn't fastened properly and all my sandwiches have dropped out!'

Take one PICNIC CARD from your LUNCHBOX. Now go to 270.

They had only gone a short way from the well when Timmy stopped at one of the trees. He had found a squirrel hole and he pushed his nose in to have a better look. 'Oh, do hurry up, Timmy,' George called back at him, 'we haven't got time to waste on squirrels!' At that very moment, though, Timmy pulled what looked like a small book out of the hole. 'Gosh, it's a codebook!' George exclaimed when she had taken it off him. 'Sorry, Timmy,' she added as she popped it into her rucksack to study later on, 'you weren't being as disobedient as I thought!'

If you don't already have it, put the CODEBOOK into your RUCKSACK. Now go to 113.

As soon as they had found the flagpost on their maps, they returned down the steps and hurried over to the grid in the ground. Anne had been correct, it *was* the cover for a hole – and a hole with steps going all the way down! 'It must be the entrance to the dungeons,' Julian said excitedly as he lifted the grid up and led the way in. ***Go to 190.***

The fisherman was right – their compasses led them to a series of narrow wooden steps set into the cliff! 'I do hope we're not too late,' said Anne as they hurriedly started to climb. The sky seemed to be growing darker by the second! *Go to 145.*

After a while, though, the man in the motor-boat said he would have to return home for his lunch and hoped they wouldn't mind if they rowed for the rest of the way. Before he left, they asked him where the best landing place was on the island. 'If you want my advice,' he replied, 'you'll avoid it altogether. But if you must land there, try the west side of the island.' As soon as he had gone, they started looking for west on their compasses.

*Use your **COMPASS CARD** to find this direction by placing exactly over the shape below – and with pointer touching north. Then go to the number that appears in the window. If you don't have a **COMPASS CARD** in your **RUCKSACK**, you'll have to guess which of the numbers to go to.*

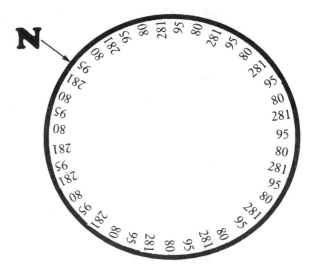

Moments after they had entered the bay, the mist suddenly cleared again! As soon as they had dragged the boat well up on to the sand so that it wouldn't be carried away, they decided to have a quick picnic to refresh themselves. 'Mm, these sandwiches of yours are just what I needed after all that rowing!' Julian told Anne appreciatively.

Take one PICNIC CARD from your LUNCHBOX. Now go to 82.

The cliffs eventually dropped down towards a small cove in the distance and they decided that's where they would land. The journey had been so exhausting that they felt they all deserved some of their picnic. As soon as they had dragged the boat up on to the beach, therefore, they opened their lunchboxes. 'It's a good job you cut so many sandwiches, Anne,' George told her. 'I feel as if I haven't eaten for a week!'

Take one PICNIC CARD from your LUNCHBOX. Now go to 82.

They hadn't quite reached the boat when disaster happened. A large wave came in and tipped it over! 'Oh no,' cried Julian, 'we didn't pull the boat up far enough. Now all our rucksacks are lying in the water!' Fortunately, the water was only a few centimetres deep and the only real damage done was to George's codebook. It had become so soggy that most of the pages fell out and it was now obviously quite useless.

If you have it, remove the CODEBOOK CARD from your RUCKSACK. Now go to 54.

Having finally agreed on George's suggestion, they all followed her towards a crumbling stone keep in the far corner of the courtyard. The inside was full of old crossbows and armour. 'This must be where the weapons were stored,' said Julian with fascination. Just as they were leaving the weapons' room and stepping out into the open again, Anne noticed a message chalked above the doorway. *ENTRANCE TO DUNGEONS IS 70 PACES DUE EAST,* it read. Thinking this might well be where the treasures were hidden, they hurriedly slipped off their rucksacks to look for their compasses!

Use your COMPASS CARD to find out which direction east is by placing exactly over the shape below – and with pointer touching north. Then go to the number that appears in the window. If you don't have a COMPASS CARD, you'll have to guess which of the numbers to go to.

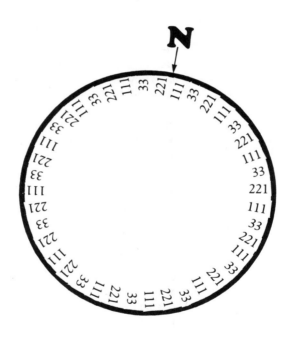

309

With Wilfrid to help them now, they at last spotted the castle – a huge mass of stone in a large clearing. Although it was in ruins, there was still a lot of it there. One tower, in fact, was almost completely undamaged! It was this tower that they decided to explore first, finding a narrow stairway that led not only up towards the top but also down into the ground. 'This down bit probably goes to the dungeons!' Dick said with an excited shiver. Thinking that's where the treasures might be hidden, they started to climb down, eventually reaching a large dark chamber at the bottom. *Go to 71.*

310

They were just about to switch their torches on when they heard footsteps coming down the stairway. 'Quick, let's hide,' said Julian, 'there's someone else here!' They managed to find their way towards some boxes, crouching down behind them. 'Hey, look, these must be treasures!' whispered Dick, putting his hand on something that felt very much like gold plates. Before he could say anything else, though, the footsteps reached the chamber and they could just make out two very unpleasant-looking men! *Go to 155.*

311

They were just taking their torches out when Anne noticed that one of the slabs in the floor was a bit wobbly. Then she saw that there was a hand-hold chiselled into it so that it could be lifted up. 'It must be the way down to the dungeons!' Dick exclaimed as they discovered a dark stairway underneath. They were in such a hurry to climb down the steps that Julian tripped and broke his bottle of ginger beer!

Take one PICNIC CARD from your LUNCHBOX. Now go to 190.

312

The coded message did indeed refer to where the treasures were hidden! It said that they could be found in some large crates at the far end of the dungeon. At last they spotted them, all opening their mouths at the gleaming gold plates and goblets inside. 'That message obviously must have been written fairly recently,' said Julian, 'because these crates are quite modern.' They were just examining one of the gold plates when they heard two men's voices coming down the steps. And they weren't very nice men, by the sound of it! 'Quick, let's crouch behind the crates,' said Julian as the voices grew louder and louder. *Go to 155.*

313

Feeling their way to the back of the cave, they noticed a large hole in the rock. 'This is it,' George exclaimed as loudly as she dare, 'this is the tunnel!' Bowing their heads, they followed the tunnel along, wondering where it would come out. 'It can't go much further, surely?' Anne asked wearily after they had been walking for a good mile or so. Finally, though, the tunnel came to an end at a large wooden door. They all had a quick gulp of ginger beer to wet their tense throats before turning the handle to see what was on the other side . . .

Take one PICNIC CARD from your LUNCHBOX. Now go to 245. (Remember: when there are no picnic cards left in your lunchbox, the game is over and you must start again.)

They hadn't been following their compasses far when Wilfrid spotted a small book wedged into the branch of a tree. 'Look, it's a codebook!' he exclaimed, tugging it out and finding lots of weird symbols inside. Realising that it probably belonged to those men, they took it with them so they wouldn't be able to use it again!

If you don't already have it, put the CODEBOOK CARD into your RUCKSACK. Now go to 12.

They had been trapped in the dungeon for quite some time when something extraordinary happened. Dick leant back against part of the damp wall and suddenly a narrow hole began to appear! 'Gosh, it seems to be some sort of secret escape route!' he exclaimed, peering in. One by one, they quietly crawled into the hole, discovering a long passage on the other side. 'It must have been made by one of the dungeon's prisoners,' Anne said as they followed it along. After a hundred metres or so, the passage narrowed down to a small hole again. Just managing to squeeze through, they found themselves half way up a vertical shaft with a long rope hanging down!

Throw the FAMOUS FIVE DICE to decide who is to climb the rope first.

JULIAN thrown	go to 90
DICK thrown	go to 23
GEORGE thrown	go to 180
ANNE thrown	go to 48
TIMMY thrown	go to 159
MYSTERY thrown	go to 131

'It doesn't seem quite so bad now,' said Anne as the torch shone across the water. Anyway, it wasn't much longer before she spotted the lights of the mainland ahead and she knew it would all be over in a few minutes. As soon as they had dragged the boat up on to the sand, they then hurriedly made their way up the cliffs and then towards the police station. 'It's a good job we had Wilfrid to direct us!' said Dick as they finally spotted the station's tiny blue light in the distance. *Go to 119.*